WHEN
PIES
FLY

WHEN PIES FLY

HANDMADE PASTRIES
*from Strudels to Stromboli,
Empanadas to Knishes*

CATHY BARROW

PHOTOGRAPHS BY CHRISTOPHER HIRSHEIMER

GRAND CENTRAL PUBLISHING

New York Boston

Grand Central Publishing
Hachette Book Group
1290 Avenue of the Americas, New York, NY 10104
grandcentrallifeandstyle.com
twitter.com/grandcentralpub

First Edition: September 2019

Grand Central Publishing is a division of Hachette
Book Group, Inc. The Grand Central Publishing name
and logo is a trademark of Hachette Book Group, Inc.

The publisher is not responsible for websites (or their
content) that are not owned by the publisher.

The Hachette Speakers Bureau provides a wide range
of authors for speaking events. To find out more, go
to www.hachettespeakersbureau.com or call (866)
376-6591.

Photographs copyright © 2019 by Hirsheimer &
Hamilton

Library of Congress Control Number: 2019939244

ISBNs: 978-1-5387-3190-1 (hardcover);
978-1-5387-3191-8 (ebook)

Printed in Canada

FRI

10 9 8 7 6 5 4 3 2 1

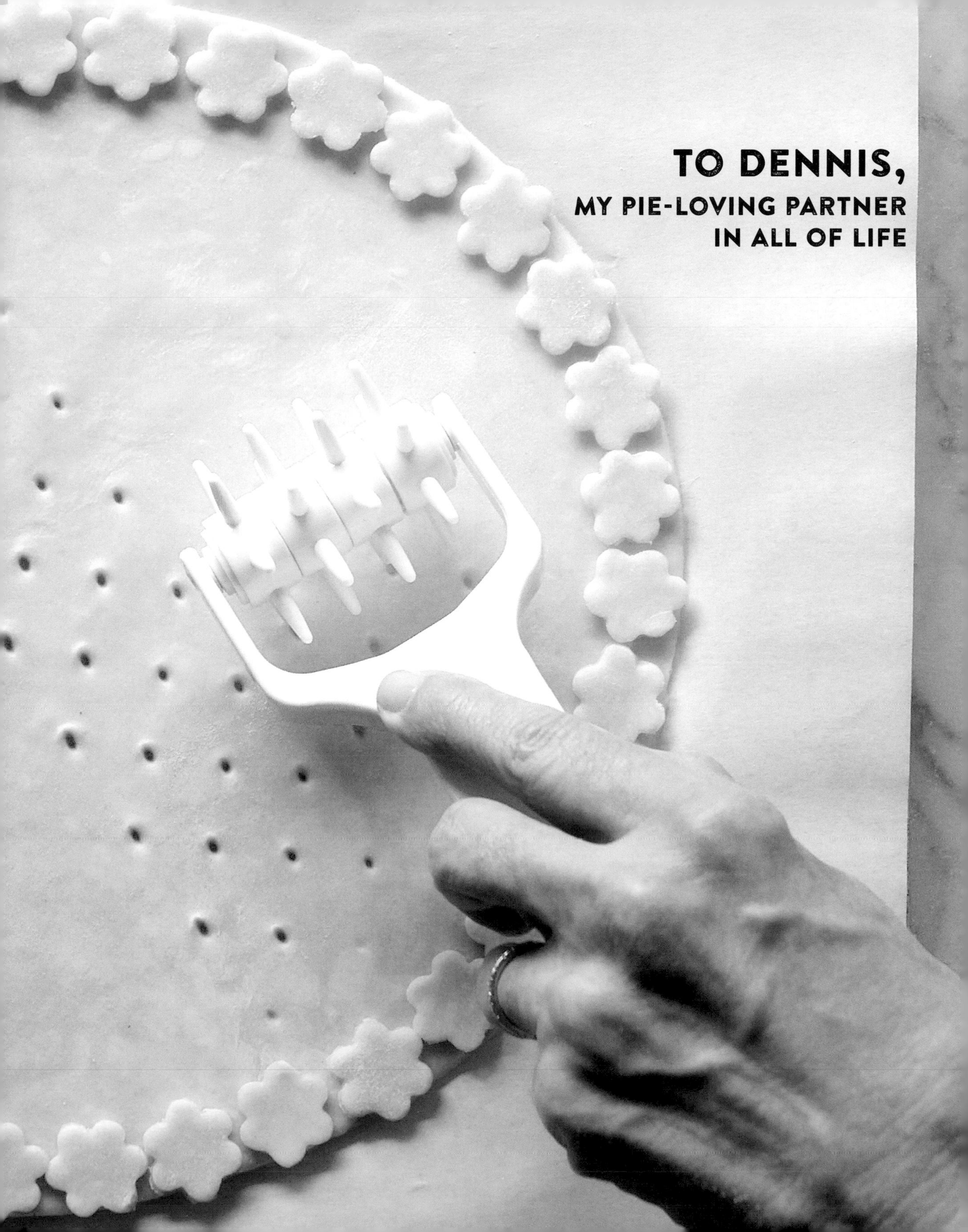

TO DENNIS,
MY PIE-LOVING PARTNER IN ALL OF LIFE

CONT

INTRODUCTION

THE AERONAUTICS OF PIE

"This is my invariable advice to people:
Learn how to cook—try new recipes, learn from your mistakes,
be fearless, and above all have fun!"

—**JULIA CHILD,** *My Life in France*

Whether sweet or savory, double crusted, scattered with toasty crumbles, intricately latticed, or with stars dotting the surface, I love a pie. I love to make pie, to eat pie, and to share pie with friends. For years, my pies were round, baked in a pie pan. I had a delicious flirtation that bloomed into an all-out love affair with square, slab pies on the way to *Pie Squared*, my first pie book.

During my slab pie year, because there were almost always blocks of pie dough or a container of filling lingering in the refrigerator, I found my mind drifting to other pie shapes and sizes. Fueled by curiosity, and because food waste weighs on me, I looked for new ways to wrap filling with pie and pastry doughs.

Home cooks around the world have faced what I call the pre-dinner scrounge since before refrigerators and plastic storage containers existed. And they have been creative with dough in almost every case. How can this leftover be refashioned, reimagined, and perhaps even stretched to fill more bellies? From this thinking, I'm now convinced, we have empanadas, filled with last night's roast, amplified into picadillo (see Turkey Picadillo Empanadas, page 181). From the imagination of cooks contemplating Northern Europe's limited winter vegetables came Onion and Sauerkraut Knishes (see page 234). And from the land of pastry itself, home cooks place a family-sized strudel on the table, bursting with vegetables and cheese, abundant and hearty (Kale, Mushroom, and Gruyère Strudel, page 142). The more I thought about the way in which we fill pastries (Spring rolls! Pasties! Samosas! Toaster pastries! Sausage rolls!) the broader the concept of flying pies became.

My view of pie became universal for anything wrapped up in pastry—a flying pie, unencumbered, not needing a pan to be formed. From the moment I imagined flying pies, I began to explore the ways different cuisines respond to that familiar refrigerator moment, staring down the options for the evening. Now, the contents of my refrigerator are regularly transformed into pies and pie-adjacent pastries.

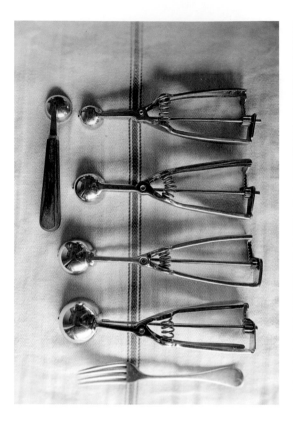

The recipes that follow are for single-serving pies to family-sized pies to party pies, both sweet and savory. There are pies for breakfast (Fresh Apricot Breakfast Pastries, page 163, and Bacon, Egg, and Swiss Hand Pies, page 33), and pies for snacks (Classic Potato Knishes, page 232, and Broccoli Cheddar Hand Pies, page 39). There are pies that make an easy dinner (Philly Cheesesteak Galette, page 13) and there are project pies (Antipasto Stromboli, page 157) that make a statement at your next potluck. More than anything, I hope you will be inspired to conjure up your own creations from the ideas I've shared on these pages.

There are seven pie doughs, virtually inter-changeable. Learn one and you'll know them all, as the same techniques result in a flaky, light, crisp crust in each recipe. And there are another six pastry doughs specific to recipes like Butter-milk Dough for Fried Fruit Pies (page 267) and Dairy-Free Dough for Knishes (page 271). Learn to make Pulled Dough for Strudel (page 262) and your dinnertime options will expand tenfold. And Quick Puff Pastry (page 265) is so different from the dough found in the grocery store, and so straightforward to make, there's a solid argument for keeping a block in the freezer all the time.

Working with any dough becomes easier with repetition. The more pie dough you roll out, the more comfortable it will become. There are specific steps for rolling out pie dough, for making strudels and knishes, for forming a *repulgue* on the edge of an empanada. I've included process photos whenever I thought they might explain the steps needed to get that pie off the ground. With practice comes proficiency. I like to remind myself that home cooks around the world make doughs regularly; it shouldn't be that big a deal.

It takes no more than imagination to dream up a pie filling, but without plenty of herbs, spices, nuts, and chiles, a filling's flavor can be overwhelmed by the richness of the pastry. I found that the smaller the pies became (see Pie Poppers, page 73), the more I had to make the fillings dynamic to deliver a big taste. It was the international aisle in the grocery store, along with my collection of cookbooks from other countries, that provided inspiration. I added fermented foods like kimchi, and used ginger, garlic, and Sriracha with abandon. It wasn't only the savory pies that benefited from this attention; sweet fillings needed coaxing, too, so I added layers of spice (Chai-Spiced Plum and Walnut Empanaditas, page 190) and texture (Strawberry Funnel Cake Pie, page 207).

Some pies demanded saucing. When I thought about Crab Rangoon Pie Poppers (page 79), I knew I had to replicate the caramel sauce that's de rigeur for that Chinese restaurant favorite. The Old-Fashioned Apple Dumpling (page 69) is delicious alone, but puddling a warm caramel sauce beneath it made me feel very fancy.

And that's really the beauty of pies. They feel a little fancy, a little special. The pages that follow are filled with shareable pies and their close cousins, knishes, kolache, strudel, and more. Bake and share these pies with your people. Pie tastes like coming home.

CHECK YOUR EQUIPMENT

A few pieces of key equipment can change up your kitchen game:

A digital **scale** makes baking better; weighing ingredients means a precise, repeatable bake.

Like a scale, an **instant read thermometer** adds precision to your kitchen game.

I can't go a day without cooking in a **cast-iron skillet.** I have 10- and 12-inch skillets, both well-loved and well-used. They were both found in sad condition at a junk shop and lovingly restored. If that's not your thing, new pans are fairly priced.

A **food processor** has been my secret weapon for decades, turning out the flakiest, most tender pie crusts. I have had an extra-large Cuisinart model for several years. The motor is strong, the blades are sharp, and the plastic parts are pretty sturdy (and easily replaced every few years, when they become scratched or chipped or lost in a house move).

A great pie has a crisp bottom crust, achieved by cooking the bottom of the pie at the same high heat as the top. I discovered the benefit of cooking atop a hot surface when I forgot to remove my beloved **Baking Steel** (see Resources, page 275) from the oven when preheating it to bake a pie. The Baking Steel is a 15-pound cast-iron slab that retains and amplifies the heat of the oven, carrying it directly to the bottom of the baking sheet holding a flying pie. A baking stone or pizza stone will work the same way, as will an inverted baking sheet, when put in the oven during preheating. It will be hot and ready for the pan holding the pie when the oven is at temperature.

Parchment paper is on the shelf at most grocery stores now, sold in rolls along with the foil and plastic wrap. For ease of use, I prefer pre-cut sheets, sized for half sheet baking sheets (13 by 18 inches) and available at kitchen shops, restaurant supply houses, and from many online retailers.

Your **rolling pin** may have handles or not, might be tapered or perfectly cylindrical. It can be silicone or wood, metal or marble. I switch between a handled silicone pin that is heavy and allows me to roll wider pieces of dough without my knuckles getting in the way and my other favorite, a heavy maple cylinder that has lived in my kitchen for about 45 years. It's smooth and heavy and familiar. Find your pin, the one that you love so much you pack it in your suitcase on the way to the vacation house.

A plastic, washable **ruler** is an essential tool. Use **painter's tape** (I like the blue because it's easily visible next to the pie dough) to mark off the size to roll out the dough—it's noted in every recipe. Then lightly dust the surface with flour and roll the dough out. It's a beautiful thing to waste less pie dough, a moment when high school geometry becomes real.

I have two different **bench scrapers,** the handled, stiff, straight-edged tool used to clean bakers' tables by scraping off the excess flour. Use the bench scraper to push

and lift as much of the dry residue as possible. The straight edge may be used to divide pie dough blocks, sure, but I also use it as a transferring tool when carrying diced onions from the cutting board to a skillet. It's a tool that is on the counter from the moment I start any kitchen project. In contrast to the stiff metal scraper, a flexible, silicone bench scraper is my favorite tool for scraping out the work bowl of the food processor, or lifting meringue from the mixing bowl to a pastry bag.

A **pastry wheel** makes ruffled edges and a **pizza wheel** makes a straight edge. In fact, a sharp paring knife will serve the same function, but I like the feeling of a handled wheel against the ruler, like an X-Acto knife against a T-square in drafting class.

Pie weights are used for blind baking (see page 100), resting atop a sheet of foil or parchment paper, and might be as simple as piles of pennies, raw dried beans, raw rice, or white sugar. (Hat tip to Stella Parks for that last one—afterward, use the toasted sugar just as you might use granulated sugar in any recipe. It delivers a distinct caramel tone.) Reusable ceramic and metal pie weights are available at kitchen shops, restaurant supply houses, and from many online retailers.

I use a **cookie scoop** to fill hand pies and poppers, empanadas, and kolache. Look for 1-tablespoon, 3-tablespoon, and ¼-cup sizes—all are smaller than a regular ice cream scoop.

An **offset spatula** has so many uses—lifting trimmed dough from the counter, swooshing frosting over a hand pie, spreading sauce along the bottom of a tart or galette. I have two sizes, small and large, and the smaller one gets more use.

For frying, for draining saucy fillings, for lifting leeks from a cool water rinse, a long-handled **skimmer**—often called a **spider**—or even a generous **slotted spoon** will be invaluable in your kitchen arsenal.

Grate cheese, garlic, ginger, or nutmeg on a **Microplane or rasp.** A **four-sided box grater** is essential for those long strands of cheese that make a melty topping.

Cookie cutters are inspiration for flying pies. Round, square, hearts, flowers, alphabet letters . . . there's no end to the options.

Small and large **silicone brushes** swab egg wash onto the top of the pie, leaving no fussy brush hairs—and they are easy to clean, too.

Find the right **cotton cloth** for strudel pulling. While a generously sized, soft, well-used, all-cotton or linen tea towel (not terry cloth) may be used for strudeling, a larger cloth like an old tablecloth—again, soft, well-worn cotton or linen—keeps the flour contained.

I love to add to my collection of **sparkling sugars, sprinkles, and other decorations.** It's especially fun to shop for these twinkling toppers when traveling in other countries. Online retailers offer many options, even color coordinated, and most grocery stores have a small collection of suitable decorations.

Recipes were developed and tested with **King Arthur** flours, grocery store "American-style" butters, and **Diamond Crystal** coarse kosher salt. Brown sugar, unless otherwise noted, refers to light brown sugar.

EARN YOUR PIE WINGS

Use a **digital kitchen scale**. Weighing ingredients guarantees the same result over and over, which is very satisfying.

All-American butter, with its higher water content, makes the best pie crust. Because I buy several pounds at a time, especially when I'm writing a book, I use Kirkland unsalted butter from Costco. If you're not buying in bulk, but a pound at a time—Breakstone, Land O'Lakes, and Horizon are all very dependable. If you use salted butter, omit the salt in the dough recipe. Save the European butter for toast and topping steamed asparagus, a bowl of creamy grits, or that warm baguette from the bakery.

Use **high-quality all-purpose flour**. I opt for King Arthur, but Gold Medal is my second favorite. It makes a difference. Unbleached flour is the norm. However, after about three days in the refrigerator, unbleached flour will contribute to the graying of unbaked pie dough. *If you know you need to make pie dough more than two days ahead or cannot freeze and defrost it two days ahead, use* <u>bleached</u> *all-purpose flour.*

Rolling a crust to a specific size will help to produce a prettier pie, one that bakes evenly. At the same time, rolling to a specific size allows the best use of the dough, particularly with hand pies and pie poppers, reducing dough waste. There's a simple trick: **Use a ruler and painter's tape** to mark a guide on the counter for the finished size of the rolled crust (see page xiv).

Egg wash (1 egg, 1 tablespoon cool water, and a big pinch of kosher salt) helps create a shiny and crackly surface that is golden brown and deeply appealing. The salt breaks down the egg, making a smoother wash without clumps, and helps it adhere.

Fillings must be entirely cold before tucking them between crusts. Hot fillings will make the crust soggy and tough.

Soggy Bottom begone. Throughout the book I recommend cooking these flying pies on a parchment-lined baking sheet that is set atop a preheated surface like a Baking Steel, baking stone, or an inverted, preheated baking sheet.

Mayonnaise, sour cream, or crème fraîche will form a barrier between the bottom crust and juicy, meaty fillings, ensuring a crisp bottom crust. Toasted bread crumbs or finely chopped nuts will form a barrier between fruity, juicy fillings and the dough.

Keep one or two blocks of **pie dough in the freezer** at all times. Pie emergencies happen.

CHAPTER 1

GALETTES

RUSTIC PIES

Galettes are friendly flying pies: Free form, open in the center, and with a no-fuss attitude, an exposed filling is embraced by rustic pleats and folds of flaky dough. They are a first-class leftover solution for last night's roast or a little bit of rotisserie chicken or a few handfuls of seasonal fruit.

A galette is a welcome, ready-in-an-instant option when there's an opportunity for pie, but there's no pie pan in sight. In the world of flying pies, galettes are at the top of the list. These free-form pies are easy-going, often round, always open-faced. There is no make-ahead strategy for galettes other than keeping pie dough on hand. Galettes should be formed, chilled, and baked all at once. They don't benefit from sitting around—as the dough warms, the weight of the filling will stretch the form. Embrace the galette as a strategy and wrap up all sorts of delicious ingredients in a rustic, appealing pie.

A RUSTIC PIE WITHOUT A PAN

Keep the fillings well-seasoned and distinctively chunky—mushy fillings will not do. Gather about 3 cups of ingredients for a 12-inch round of dough, to fill, but not overfill, the galette. A balanced ratio of dough to filling is preferred, about the same as a sandwich served on hearty bread. It was with sandwiches in mind that I conjured up savory options like Roast Turkey, Leek, and Gouda Galette (page 9) and Philly Cheesesteak Galette (page 13).

The sweet galettes are mostly fruity, because there's nothing as charming as piling up beautiful, slightly sugared, positively ripe, highly scented, summer berries and lovingly pleating a buttery dough around them. These beauties rely on the bounty of the market and a devil-may-care attitude. These are guidelines more than recipes and changing up blackberry to marionberry in the Bumbleberry Galette (page 24) is as easy as pie. With the Blackberry Peach Galette (page 21), use the weights suggested and trade peaches for blueberries for nectarines for cherries for blackberries for raspberries for apricots.

THE RIGHT CRUST

Crusts make the galette, so do not feel restricted to the specific dough suggested in each recipe. Swap doughs at will. Cream Cheese (page 252) instead of All-Butter (page 251). Everything Spice (page 257) instead of Caramelized Onion and Cheese (page 259). Brown-Butter (page 254) for, well, anything. Feel inspired and encouraged to let your galette fly.

Keep the dough cold. Roll your round out to ¼ inch thick, no more than 12 inches across. If the dough is too thin, the galette will spring a leak. Work quickly. If the dough warms at all, the pleating will suffer, and the shape won't hold, so chill the dough after rolling, using the time to construct the filling. A lava flow of all those lovely ingredients is a crying shame, but a whisper of filling enthusiastically bubbling up is a thrill. The recipes for pie crusts can be found on pages 251 to 259.

FILLINGS THAT STAY ON COURSE

It's possible to make a galette in no time at all, once the filling is prepared. The filling must be cold to help the form stay put. Work quickly and with a cold dough disk. Pile the filling in the middle of the rolled out round and gather up the edges as though forming a bundle. Fold evenly spaced pleats that make a tidy package about 7 or 8 inches across at the base.

Because of the weight of the filling and the elasticity of the dough, it is likely a galette will spread and open up while cooking. This is only a problem if the pleats give way and the galette flattens and the filling spills out. To avoid this problem, lift 2 to 3 inches of the edge up and over the filling, enthusiastically pinch the pleats together,

and encourage the filling to move and fill in the tidy form with no large air pockets.

Some fillings are juicy, like the Blackberry Peach Galette (page 21), so I like to lift out the solids with a slotted spoon and reserve the liquid until the formed galette has chilled. I add back the juices right before I slide the galette into the oven, using a cup measure with a pouring spout to direct that delicious liquid into the center of the galette. This helps control overflow while ensuring a juicy filling.

A FIRM UNDERPINNING

Bake the galette on a baking sheet on top of a hot surface. I like the Baking Steel, but a baking stone or an inverted baking sheet, heated along with the oven, will also provide the sizzling hot surface that encourages a crispy bottom crust. Galettes should slice cleanly from top to bottom, with a tidy form and no soggy dough.

CARRY ON

Chill the galette for 30 to 45 minutes after forming it. At the very least, put it in the refrigerator for 15 minutes.

Fillings should not be runny, but also should not be dry. It's a paradox. Think saucy, cooking down fillings until they are glazed with the sauce. And protect the crisp bottom crust by including a barrier, like mayonnaise or crème fraîche for the savory pies, or nuts or bread crumbs for the sweet ones.

Fillings must be boldly seasoned. Be confident with herbs, spices, salt, and pepper.

Roll the dough to ¼-inch thickness. It's easier to manage when it isn't too thin.

Don't let the edges get too thin. Avoid rolling over the edge of the dough, or simply trim the dough round back to a thicker edge before lifting and pleating.

Let the galette rest. Savory galettes should be removed from the oven and allowed to rest for a few minutes before serving. Fruit galettes should cool for 2 hours or more to give the filling time to set up. If it's warm fruit pie you want, reheat the galette briefly in a 350°F oven.

Keep a watchful eye. If the crust looks like it's browning too quickly, gently tent the entire pie with foil until it's finished baking. The Caramelized Onion and Cheese Pie Dough (page 259) and the Brown-Butter Pie Dough (page 254), especially, as each has a tendency to brown more quickly.

QUICHE LORETTA GALETTE

Serves 8

---

1 recipe All-Butter Pie Dough, page 251, formed into a disk

---

1 pound (450 g) ripe tomatoes (3 or 4 medium)

½ teaspoon kosher salt

2 large eggs

2 tablespoons (1 ounce, 28 g) cream cheese, at room temperature

¾ cup (85 g) sliced, chopped, or shaved country ham (see headnote)

½ cup (50 g) sliced scallions, white and green parts (about 4)

½ teaspoon dry mustard, preferably Coleman's

½ teaspoon freshly ground pepper

4 ounces (113 g) extra sharp cheddar cheese, shredded on the largest holes of a box grater (about 1 cup)

¼ cup (56 g) mayonnaise

⅔ cup (28 g) fresh bread crumbs

Egg wash (1 egg beaten with 1 tablespoon cool water and ¼ teaspoon kosher salt)

I love a classic Southern tomato pie and I love quiche Lorraine, that hammy, cheesy, Paris-bistro treat. So it's little wonder I created this galette, a sunny mash-up of the two. Country ham is deeply flavored, an American version of prosciutto, but baked ham will work as well. If substituting baked ham, increase the salt by ¼ teaspoon. Delicious warm or at room temperature and served with a salad, this is a satisfying supper.

Line a baking sheet with parchment. Remove the dough from the refrigerator and allow it to warm slightly. Roll out the disk to a 12-inch round and, wrapping the dough lightly around the rolling pin, lift and place it on the baking sheet. Cover and refrigerate while you make the filling.

Tomatoes are juicy and can contribute to a soggy pie. Cut them in half, scoop out and discard the gel and seeds, and roughly chop them. Place in a colander, combine with ½ teaspoon salt, and let the moisture drain from the tomatoes for 15 minutes.

In the bowl of the stand mixer, beat the eggs and cream cheese until combined. It will not be totally smooth. Stir in the ham, scallions, dry mustard, and pepper. Combine ½ cup of the cheese with the mayonnaise in a small bowl. Combine the chopped, thoroughly drained tomatoes with the bread crumbs.

Spread the mayonnaise/cheese mixture across the center of the dough round, leaving a 2-inch border. Layer on the tomato/bread crumbs and then the ham mixture. Top with the remaining ½ cup cheese.

Lift the outside edges of the dough and pull them up and slightly over the filling, leaving the center exposed. Work your way around the galette, folding the dough over on itself and forming a series of pleats (see photo, page 3) that make a

snug little package. The center of the galette should be open, but there should also be a very distinct crusty edge holding in the filling. Brush the galette with the egg wash.

Chill the galette for 45 minutes.

Place a Baking Steel, baking stone, or inverted baking sheet on the center rack and heat the oven to 400°F. Slide the baking sheet with the galette onto the hot stone, steel, or sheet and bake for 35 to 40 minutes, until the filling is bubbling and the crust is deeply browned. Cool slightly before serving.

ROAST TURKEY, LEEK, AND GOUDA GALETTE

Serves 8

1 recipe Everything Spice Pie Dough, page 257, formed into a disk

2 leeks, pale green and white parts only, sliced in ¼-inch-thick disks (about 1 cup, 450 g)

8 tablespoons (4 ounces, 113 g) cream cheese, cut into small cubes

8 ounces (225 g) aged gouda, shredded (about 2 cups)

1 tablespoon minced fresh chives

1 tablespoon minced fresh flat-leaf parsley

½ teaspoon minced fresh thyme leaves

½ teaspoon kosher salt

½ teaspoon freshly ground black pepper

4 slices (4 ounces, 113 g) thick-cut smoked bacon, chopped*

12 ounces (340 g) cooked turkey or Easiest Roast Turkey Breast (recipe follows), cubed (about 2 cups)

Egg wash (1 egg beaten with 1 tablespoon cool water and ¼ teaspoon kosher salt)

* **NOTE:** Not needed if your turkey is from the Easiest Roast Turkey Breast recipe.

After a holiday meal, there's always a little bit of turkey hanging around. Tuck it into this flavorful pie reminiscent of a favorite deli sandwich. Even if it's months until Turkey Day, consider roasting a turkey breast (recipe follows): Not only will the house smell terrific, a turkey dinner is always welcome, and it can lead to this satisfying pie.

Line a baking sheet with parchment. Remove the dough from the refrigerator and allow it to warm slightly. Roll out the dough to a 12-inch round and place on the baking sheet. Cover and refrigerate while making the filling.

Fill a large mixing bowl with cold water. Add the sliced leeks and stir them around with your hand. Let any dirt fall to the bottom of the bowl, then scoop the leeks off the top and drain on a clean kitchen towel. Roll up the leeks to further dry them and set aside.

Line a plate with paper towels. Cook the bacon in a large skillet over medium heat, stirring occasionally, until crisp. Transfer the bacon to the paper towels. If there is more than a tablespoon of fat in the pan, pour it off.

Add the leeks to the pan and let them cook, undisturbed, until wilted, about 5 minutes. Scrape the leeks into a large bowl and add the cream cheese, gouda, chives, parsley, thyme, salt, and pepper to the bowl. Add the chopped bacon to the bowl. Stir gently to combine, then add the turkey and stir until everything is evenly distributed. Spread the filling out on a baking sheet, cover, and refrigerate to chill it for about 20 minutes. If making well ahead, cover the bowl, and refrigerate.

(Continued)

Spoon the filling into the center of the dough. Lift the outside edges of the dough and pull them up and slightly over the filling, leaving the center exposed. Work your way around the galette, folding the dough over on itself and forming a series of pleats that make a snug little package (see photo, page 3). The center of the galette should be open, but there should also be a very distinct crusty edge to hold in the filling. Brush the galette with the egg wash.

Chill the galette for 45 minutes.

Place a Baking Steel, baking stone, or inverted baking sheet on the center rack and heat the oven to 400°F. Slide the baking sheet with the galette onto the hot stone, steel, or sheet and bake for 35 to 40 minutes, until the filling is bubbling and the crust is deeply browned.

EASIEST ROAST TURKEY BREAST

Makes more than enough for 1 galette

1 (3-pound, 1.4-kg) boneless turkey breast, tied for roasting

1 tablespoon cracked black pepper

½ pound (225 g) thick-sliced smoked bacon

A roast turkey breast is a great way to start the week. Make it on Sunday and you'll have the Roast Turkey, Leek, and Gouda Galette to look forward to later in the week, as well as sandwiches, tacos, curries, and more. There is no need to secure the bacon, it's going to infuse the turkey meat with delicious smoky flavor while it's simply draped across the top like an odalisque. I use the best bacon I can find, locally cured and smoked, which tends to be less salty than commercial bacon. (To avoid an overly salty filling if using a commercially produced bacon, add only half the bacon to the accompanying galette recipe.)

Use a thermometer for no surprises. Turkey breasts, like turkeys, come in all different sizes. This recipe may be scaled up, mathematically adjusted to suit whatever size turkey breast you find at the store. For timing, a good rule of thumb is to cook a boneless, rolled, and tied turkey breast for 20 to 25 minutes per pound, to an internal temperature of 165°F.

Heat the oven to 350°F. Place the turkey breast on a parchment-lined baking sheet. Rub the pepper all over the surface and then drape the bacon slices over the turkey. Roast for 60 to 75 minutes, until the internal temperature measures 165°F.

Remove from the oven and cool for 15 minutes before slicing. If you are making the Roast Turkey, Leek, and Gouda Galette, remove the bacon and chop it for the filling. When preparing the turkey for the galette, first slice 1-inch slabs and then dice the slabs into 1-inch cubes.

PHILLY CHEESESTEAK GALETTE

Serves 8

1 recipe Caramelized Onion and Cheese Pie Dough, page 259, formed into a disk

8 ounces (225 g) cooked steak or roast beef, preferably rare or medium-rare

2 tablespoons olive oil

8 ounces (225 g) cremini mushrooms, sliced (2 generous cups)

2 medium onions (450 g, 1 pound), sliced into ¼-inch-thick half-moons (3 cups)

1½ cups (360 ml) heavy cream

5 ounces (140 g) provolone, shredded (1½ cups)

1 large egg yolk

1 teaspoon kosher salt

½ teaspoon freshly ground black pepper

2 tablespoons mayonnaise

1 tablespoon pickled hot peppers, sliced (optional)

Egg wash (1 egg beaten with 1 tablespoon cool water and ¼ teaspoon kosher salt)

Roasted mushrooms, griddled onions, and tender steak—this pie has every element of the sandwich so ubiquitous in the City of Brotherly Love. It's the perfect pie to extend the leftovers from a roast, the last bits of a steak, or deli roast beef. *Fonduta*, a pale, gooey, creamy cheese sauce fortified with an egg yolk, ties the whole thing together. I love the spike of hot pickled peppers on the top, but if your family shies away from the heat, just omit them, or griddle one sliced red or green bell pepper with the onions and add it to the filling. The onion and cheese crust takes this pie right over the top.

Line a baking sheet with parchment. Remove the dough from the refrigerator and allow it to warm slightly. Roll out the dough to a 12-inch round and place on the baking sheet. Cover and refrigerate while making the filling.

Slice the meat into thin ribbons or bite-sized pieces. Heat 1 tablespoon of the olive oil in a large skillet over medium-high heat. When it shimmers, add the mushrooms and let them cook, undisturbed, until deeply browned, about 6 minutes. Shake the pan to loosen the mushrooms—if they stick, continue cooking until they release with a shake—and brown the other side in the same manner, about 3 minutes longer. Remove to a bowl. Add the remaining 1 tablespoon oil to the pan and then add the onions. Cook for about 12 minutes, until wilted, softened, sweet, and beginning to turn golden brown on the edges. Add to the bowl with the mushrooms.

Gently boil the cream in a medium saucepan over medium-high heat until reduced by one-half, about 30 minutes. When it first begins to boil, it will foam actively and threaten to boil over. Just take the pan off the heat, stir, and return to the heat, stirring constantly. After the initial foaming, it will settle back into a bubbly slow boil, cooking down and thickening in about 30 minutes. Remove from the heat and whisk in the cheese, egg yolk, salt, and pepper. Stir the cream mixture into the onion and mushroom mixture.

Spread the mayonnaise across the dough, leaving a 1-inch border. Scatter the steak evenly across the mayonnaise and pile the onion and mushroom mixture on top of the steak. Lift the outside edges of the dough and pull them up and slightly over the filling, leaving the center exposed. Work your way around the galette, folding the dough over itself and forming a series of pleats that make a snug little package (see photo, page 3). The center of the galette should be open, but there should also be a very distinct crusty edge to hold in the filling.

Chill the galette for 45 minutes.

Place a Baking Steel, baking stone, or inverted baking sheet on the center rack and heat the oven to 400°F. Slide the baking sheet with the galette onto the hot stone, steel, or sheet and bake for 40 minutes, until the filling is bubbling and the crust is deeply browned. Cool slightly before serving warm, with pickled peppers on top if you like.

HOT CRAB DIP GALETTE

Serves 8 to 10

1 recipe Cream Cheese Pie Dough, page 252, formed into a disk

---

1 tablespoon grapeseed, canola, or another neutral oil

2 tablespoons minced shallot

8 ounces (225 g) chopped frozen spinach, defrosted and squeezed dry (about ½ cup)

8 tablespoons (4 ounces, 113 g) cream cheese, softened, cubed

½ cup (113 g) crème fraîche or mayonnaise

2 tablespoons Old Bay seasoning

1 teaspoon dry mustard

½ cup (56 g) shredded cheddar cheese

1 cup (140 g) chopped squeezed-dry canned artichoke hearts in water

½ pound (225 g) fresh crabmeat, picked over for any stray shell or cartilage

---

Egg wash (1 egg beaten with 1 tablespoon cool water and ¼ teaspoon kosher salt)

Hot sauce, for serving

Living in the mid-Atlantic has made me a fan of all things crab. I've eaten eggs Chesapeake (with crab standing in for Benedict's ham), I've tucked into stuffed nuggets of crab in tacos and salads, and I've spent more than a few hours hunkered over a picnic table piled with generously spiced crabs and cold beer. For this galette, I relied on a classic recipe for Maryland crab dip, a cheesy, gooey, delightful way to scoop crab onto a cracker. With a pie, there's no cracker necessary—instead the dip is nestled in a tender crust for a very rich, decadent appetizer, or lunch with a salad on the side. I've included spinach because we all need more vegetables in our life, and the greens add a vegetal snap to the combination as well as a nice spark of color.

Line a baking sheet with parchment. Remove the dough from the refrigerator and allow it to warm slightly. Roll out the dough to a 12-inch round and place on the baking sheet. Cover and refrigerate while making the filling.

Heat the oil in a large wide skillet over medium-high heat until shimmering. Add the shallot and cook until wilted, about 3 minutes. Add the spinach and cook until dry, another 3 to 5 minutes.

In a large bowl, combine the cream cheese, crème fraîche, Old Bay, and mustard using a sturdy spoon, stirring well and thoroughly until smooth. Fold in the spinach mixture, cheddar, artichoke hearts, and crabmeat.

Pile the crabmeat mixture into the center of the dough. Lift the outside edges of the dough and pull them up and slightly over the filling, leaving the center exposed. Work your way around the galette, folding the dough over on itself and forming a series of pleats that make a snug little package (see photo, page 3). The center of the galette should be open, but there should also be a very distinct crusty edge to hold in the filling. Paint the galette with the egg wash.

Chill the galette for 45 minutes.

Place a Baking Steel, baking stone, or inverted baking sheet on the center rack and heat the oven to 400°F. Slide the baking sheet with the galette onto the hot stone, steel, or sheet and bake for 35 to 40 minutes, until the filling is bubbling. Serve hot with hot sauce, for those who are so inclined.

RHUBARB BERRY GALETTE

Serves 8 to 10

---

1 recipe All-Butter Pie Dough, page 251, formed into a disk

⅔ cup (135 g) granulated sugar

¼ cup (38 g) finely chopped crystallized ginger

3 tablespoons cornstarch

¼ teaspoon ground cardamom

¼ teaspoon ground ginger

⅛ teaspoon freshly grated nutmeg

12 ounces (340 g) rhubarb, sliced into ½-inch chunks (2 cups)

1 cup (125 g) strawberries, hulled and quartered

1 teaspoon lemon juice

1 cup (125 g) raspberries

½ cup (21 g) fresh bread crumbs

1 tablespoon (14 g) unsalted butter, cubed and chilled

Egg wash (1 egg beaten with 1 tablespoon cool water and ¼ teaspoon kosher salt)

Sparkling sugar

Rhubarb is a glorious harbinger of summer. If you grow it, you know the majesty of the plant with giant leaves that unfurl in early summer. But even if you've never seen it spring from the earth, there's the way that the ruby red stalks shine at the farmers' market. Rhubarb adds both heft and color to a pie filling, as well as a pucker-worthy tartness that benefits from the addition of a few sweet berries for balance. The bread crumbs will help with potential runniness. Serve this galette for breakfast. Yes, I said it. Just make a pie for breakfast. It's nothing more than a bowl-shaped pie crust filled with fruit.

Line a baking sheet with parchment. Remove the dough from the refrigerator and allow it to warm slightly. Roll out the dough to a 12-inch round and place on the baking sheet. Cover and refrigerate while making the filling.

Whisk the granulated sugar, crystallized ginger, cornstarch, cardamom, ground ginger, and nutmeg together. Add the rhubarb, strawberries, lemon juice, and lastly, very gently, the raspberries.

Scatter the bread crumbs across the center of the dough round, leaving a 2-inch border. Scrape out the filling and any accumulated juices into the center of the round. Lift the outside edges of the dough and pull them up and slightly over the filling, leaving the center exposed. Work your way around the galette, folding the dough over on itself and forming a series of pleats that make a snug little package (see photo, page 3). The center of the galette should be open, but there should also be a very distinct crusty edge to hold in the filling. Brush the galette with the egg wash and sprinkle the sparkling sugar generously over the surface.

Chill the galette for 45 minutes.

(Continued)

Place a Baking Steel, baking stone, or inverted baking sheet on the center rack and heat the oven to 400°F. Slide the baking sheet with the galette onto the hot stone, steel, or sheet and bake for 35 to 40 minutes, until the filling is bubbling and the crust is deeply golden brown. Cool for an hour or more on a wire rack. This celebration of summer deserves ice cream.

BLACKBERRY PEACH GALETTE

Serves 8

1 recipe All-Butter Pie Dough, page 251, formed in a disk

———

½ cup (100 g) granulated sugar

3 tablespoons cornstarch

2 (2-inch) swaths lime zest, removed with a vegetable peeler, avoiding the white pith

Juice of 1 lime

2 cups (170 g) peeled and pitted peaches, chopped into 1-inch cubes (about 3 to 4 medium)

3 sprigs fresh mint

1 cup (120 g) blackberries

½ cup (21 g) fresh bread crumbs

1 tablespoon (14 g) unsalted butter, cold and cubed

———

Egg wash (1 egg beaten with 1 tablespoon cool water and ¼ teaspoon kosher salt)

Sparkling sugar

The thing about berry pies is the filling gets even better if it has some time to hang out and develop. Adding herbs, citrus, booze, or spices will amplify the berry flavor in a heady treatment that makes a galette just a little more special, but it also leads to a very juicy galette, likely to leak. Here blackberries and peaches combine in one of the quintessential flavor duets of summer's symphony. I give the filling a boost with mint and lime, steeping them with the peaches for a quick flavor injection. Separate the fruit from the juices for the first chill, then pour the juices in just before the galette goes into the oven. I like to use a glass cup measure with a spout for this.

Line a baking sheet with parchment. Remove the dough from the refrigerator and allow it to warm slightly. Roll out the dough to a 12-inch round and place on the baking sheet. Cover and refrigerate while making the filling.

Whisk the granulated sugar, cornstarch, and lime zest and juice together in a large bowl. Gently fold in the peaches and mint, stirring until the sugar has dissolved. Cover with plastic wrap and let the filling sit for 1 hour on the counter. Remove and discard the mint sprigs and lime zest. Gently stir in the blackberries, so they aren't crushed.

Scatter the bread crumbs across the center of the dough round, leaving a 2-inch border. Lift the fruit out of the bowl using a slotted spoon, leaving all the juices behind, and place in the center of the dough round. Reserve the juices. Scatter the butter over the top of the fruit. Lift the outside edges of the dough and pull them up and slightly over the filling, leaving the center exposed. Work your way around the galette, folding the dough over on itself and forming a series of pleats that make a snug little package (see photo, page 3). The center of the galette should be open, but there also should be a very distinct crusty edge to hold in the filling. Brush the galette with the egg wash and sprinkle sparkling sugar generously over the surface.

Chill the galette for 30 minutes.

Place a Baking Steel, baking stone, or inverted baking sheet on the center rack and heat the oven to 400°F. Pour the reserved juices into the center of the galette. Slide the baking sheet with the galette onto the hot stone, steel, or sheet and bake for 35 to 40 minutes, until the filling is bubbling and the crust is deeply golden brown. Cool for an hour or more before serving. Try a little scoop of crème fraîche on the side.

BUMBLEBERRY GALETTE

Serves 8

1 recipe All-Butter Pie Dough, page 251, formed into a disk

___

½ to ¾ cup (100 to 150 g) granulated sugar, depending on how sweet and juicy the berries are

3 tablespoons cornstarch

3 cups (360 g) mixed berries; my favorite mix is red currants, blueberries, and raspberries

1 tablespoon lemon juice

1 tablespoon elderflower liqueur, crème de violette, or Grand Marnier (optional)

½ cup (21 g) fresh bread crumbs

2 tablespoons (28 g) unsalted butter, cold and cubed

___

Egg wash (1 egg beaten with 1 tablespoon cool water and ¼ teaspoon kosher salt)

Sparkling sugar

Bumbleberry was unknown to me until my friend Marilyn, who travels to Minnesota's lakes every summer, shared a photograph of a pie shop chalkboard listing their pies. Bumbleberry captured my attention—it's not a berry, it's any combination of three berries. What follows is more road map than recipe, and I encourage you to combine at will: blueberries, raspberries, blackberries, huckleberries, mulberries, marionberries, gooseberries, or currants. But never thuggish strawberries. I like my berry pies tart, so I hew toward less sugar, but if you prefer a sweeter berry filling, add the greater amount of sugar. This galette is likely to bubble over and leak onto the parchment lined baking sheet. Embrace the flood.

Line a baking sheet with parchment. Remove the dough from the refrigerator and allow it to warm slightly. Roll out the dough to an 11-inch round and place on the baking sheet. Cover and refrigerate while making the filling.

Whisk the granulated sugar and cornstarch together in a large bowl. Gently fold in the berries, then squeeze the lemon juice over the top and stir until the sugar has dissolved. Sprinkle with the liqueur.

Scatter the bread crumbs across the center of the dough, leaving a 2-inch border. Scrape out the berry filling into the center of the dough round and scatter the butter cubes over the top. Work quickly: Lift the outside edges of the dough and pull them up and slightly over the filling, leaving the center exposed. Work your way around the galette, folding the dough over on itself and forming a series of pleats that make a snug little package (see photo, page 3). The center of the galette should be open, but there should also be a very distinct crusty edge to hold in the filling. Brush the edge

with the egg wash and sprinkle sparkling sugar generously over the surface.

Chill the galette for 30 to 45 minutes.

Place a Baking Steel, baking stone, or inverted baking sheet on the center rack and heat the oven to 400°F. Slide the baking sheet with the galette onto the hot stone, steel, or sheet and bake for 35 to 40 minutes, until the filling is bubbling and the crust is deeply golden brown. Cool for an hour or more before serving.

CHOCOLATE PECAN TASSIE GALETTE

Serves 8

1 batch Brown-
Butter Pie Dough,
page 254, formed
into a disk

1½ cups
(170 g) pecans

¼ cup (53 g)
packed brown
sugar

2 tablespoons
(1 ounce, 28 g)
cream cheese

1 tablespoon
(14 g) unsalted
butter, softened

1 large egg

2 tablespoons
maple syrup

2 tablespoons
bourbon

½ teaspoon
kosher salt

3 ounces
(85 g) bittersweet
chocolate,
chopped
(about ½ cup)

Egg wash
(1 egg beaten
with 1 tablespoon
cool water and
¼ teaspoon
kosher salt)

Chocolate and pecans go together, sure, but add a touch of bourbon and the combination soars to the flavor stratosphere. The brown-butter crust doubles up on the toasty nuttiness. Or opt for a chocolate crust—totally over the top. Go ahead and switch to semisweet chocolate if you prefer it to bittersweet.

Remove the dough from the refrigerator and allow it to warm slightly. Line a baking sheet with parchment. Roll out the pie dough to a 12-inch round and place on the baking sheet. Cover and refrigerate while making the filling.

Scatter the pecans across a second baking sheet and toast the nuts until scented, 8 to 10 minutes. Transfer the nuts to a cutting board, let them cool, then roughly chop.

In the work bowl of a stand mixer, beat the brown sugar, cream cheese, and butter until thick and creamy. Add the egg and beat until smooth. Stir in the maple syrup, bourbon, and salt. With a stiff spatula, fold in the pecans and chocolate.

Pile the nut mixture into the center of the dough round. Lift the outside edges of the dough and pull them up and slightly over the filling, leaving the center exposed. Work your way around the galette, folding the dough over on itself and forming a series of pleats that make a snug little package (see photo, page 3). The center of the galette should be open, but there should also be a very distinct crusty edge to hold in the filling. Brush the galette with the egg wash. Chill the galette for 45 minutes.

Place a Baking Steel, baking stone, or inverted baking sheet on the center rack and heat the oven to 400°F. Slide the baking sheet with the galette onto the hot stone, steel, or sheet and bake for 45 to 55 minutes, until the filling is bubbling and the crust is deeply browned.

Cool before serving to allow the filling to set up.

CHAPTER 2

HAND PIES AND MORE

SINGLE-SERVING PIES

In Poldark's Cornwall, silver miners carried pasties to work, hot out of the oven. These meaty lunchtime treats were, quite literally, made to heat the pockets of the miners during the day, the forerunner to today's hand pies. Savory or sweet, here is a collection of flying pies, individually sized.

and pies are a little tricky. To avoid dough waste, they require levels of precision; to keep their form, they need multiple rounds of chilling and a light touch when filling. But they are so worth it. They are dessert for all the kids, no plates necessary. They are an easy, fortifying meal in a tidy package. Or they are breakfast on the run. Also in this chapter: individual lemon tartlettes and evocative little apple dumplings—two stars of the buffet table. Hand pies are the freezer-friendly, what's-for-dinner solution for today's busy household.

BOLD FILLINGS

Hand pies, by their very nature, have a quirky filling-to-crust ratio. There's scant filling and lots of pastry, requiring a balance that's very different from a galette or a round (or slab) pie. But like a private jet that seats only four, this is the right vehicle for the very rich (fillings)—like Kalbi Short Rib Hand Pies (page 47) or Cheeseburger Hand Pies (page 45). In these recipes, the filling is sturdy, textural, spiced, and big flavored to accommodate the surrounding pastry.

When making the filling, taste carefully. If it doesn't make you sit up and pay attention, I encourage salting with flair or adding a dash more pepper, spice, or hot sauce, or a squeeze of lemon juice or maybe a nubbin of butter—whatever you need to amplify the nuanced flavors and help the filling stand out in its pastry pillow.

FORMING, CRIMPING, AND VENTING HAND PIES

While a hand pie can be almost any shape, I've made most of these rectangular, in order to make the most of the pie dough. Hand pies are notoriously wasteful of dough, but I was determined to bust that reputation. The pie doughs for hand pies may be found on pages 251 to 259.

Roll out one block of dough to 11 by 11 inches and ⅛ inch thick (see Rolling, page 247), then cut twelve 3½- by 2½-inch rectangles.

A proper venting hole in the top crust is essential. The filling expands as it warms and if the vent is too small, the top crust will lift right off the bottom. Cut about a ½-inch vent in the middle of six of the rectangles (these will be the top crusts) using a tiny fondant cutter, a very small cookie cutter, or the smaller end of a pastry tip, making sure the hole remains open when the hand pie is topped. The opening is likely to stretch as you cover the filling, so keep the initial vent small. Place the forms on a baking sheet and chill for at least 20 minutes before filling. In fact, just get in the habit of chilling at every step along the way. Working with cold dough is always easier.

Working with cold filling and forming one pie at a time, brush the edges on one of the rectangles with the egg wash. Place a scant ¼ cup filling in the center of the rectangle. I like to use a scoop for portioning. It compacts the filling, which helps to ensure enough filling gets into the hand pie.

Lift a vented rectangle and place over the filling, covering the bottom rectangle. Work your way around the pie, pinching the edges closed while also releasing any air bubbles around the filling. I like to hold the bottom rectangle in my palm and form the pie in my hand. Others like to work on the board. You will find what is most comfortable for you.

Transfer the hand pie to the baking sheet and crimp the edges with a fork. Repeat until there

are six crimped pies on the baking sheet, then chill them while repeating the process with the other block of pie dough.

To help the pies keep their shape in baking, freeze or refrigerate the unbaked pies for at least 30 minutes. I find it takes about that long to roll out, cut, and form six hand pies, so I put one batch in the oven when the next batch is ready to be placed in the freezer.

The recipes that follow yield 12 hand pies (using two blocks of dough), but if you (like me) revel in big batch cooking, I suggest making a double batch, or making two or three hand pie recipes at once, placing extras in the freezer, either baked or unbaked. Some night after work, when it's dark and cold, you are going to thank me.

STORING, FREEZING, AND REHEATING

Make space in your freezer now. If your household is occasionally chaotic, like mine, a stash of satisfying pies makes life a little easier. Bacon, Egg, and Swiss Hand Pies (page 33) are sure to be more delicious than any grab-and-go breakfast at the deli, after all.

Hand pies may be frozen before or after baking. Place the pies apart on a baking sheet lined with parchment and place in the freezer for about

40 minutes, until solid. This first freeze will help them keep their shape. Then place them in a zip-top freezer bag and store in the freezer. The pies will remain delicious for 3 months.

The only hand pies that cannot be successfully frozen are the Mocha Cream Hand Pies (page 61), as pastry cream does not freeze. The other sweet hand pies, Bet-You-a-Blueberry (page 55) and Brown Sugar–Cinnamon (page 57), should not be frosted before freezing.

To bake frozen unbaked pies, follow the directions in the original recipe. The pies bake for the same amount of time, frozen or not, but check for the usual visual clues like a golden-brown crust and signs of a bubbling filling to be sure. Test to determine the filling is hot by plunging a metal knife into the center and carefully touching the tip of the knife. Is it warm? If not continue to warm the pie for another 5 minutes or so.

To reheat already baked hand pies, loosely wrap each in foil and pop in a 350°F oven (or the toaster oven at the office!) until heated through, about 15 minutes. Use the metal knife test, above, to determine whether the filling is hot. If not, continue to warm the pie for another 5 to 10 minutes.

CARRY ON

If the filling is oozing out of the edges of the hand pie, check the venting hole—it likely needs to be slightly larger.

If the filling is volcano-ing out of the tops of the hand pies, check the venting hole—it likely needs to be slightly smaller.

Glue **the pastry together with egg wash,** then crimp hard with a fork, your fingers, or any decorating tool to seal. A firm seal is vital to the structure of the pie.

Do not overfill hand pies or the crimp will not hold. Use a scant ¼ cup, or generous 3 tablespoons, of filling. A scoop is very helpful because it compacts the filling and it's easier to fit and form the top crust over a tidy filling.

Tough crust? **Make sure the filling is cold** and the dough doesn't warm as you stretch it over the filling. It is helpful to freeze the hand pies before baking to improve flake and reduce the possibility of a chewy crust.

Taste the filling before forming the hand pie. It should be boldly flavored.

Bake until really deeply golden brown or risk limp pies. A hand pie must be crisp to be delicious and easy to eat.

BACON, EGG, AND SWISS HAND PIES

Makes 12

6 slices
(6 ounces, 170 g)
thick-cut smoked
bacon, diced

6 large eggs

2 tablespoons
cool water

¼ teaspoon
herbes de
Provence

½ teaspoon
kosher salt

¼ teaspoon
freshly ground
black pepper

½ cup
(56 g) shredded
Jarlsberg or
another firm
Swiss-style
cheese

3 tablespoons
chopped fresh
chives

2 recipes
Everything Spice
Pie Dough, page
257, formed into
square blocks

Egg wash
(1 egg beaten
with 1 tablespoon
cool water and
¼ teaspoon
kosher salt)

An egg sandwich is a familiar way to start the day and an egg sandwich pie is all that—and more. Fluffy scrambled eggs and nutty melted cheese, with the crunch of bacon: This combo gets engines started all across the United States. Slightly undercook the eggs for silky, tender curds in the final pie. Easy to heat and eat, here's the ideal breakfast for all the on-the-go people in your household.

Line a dinner plate with paper towels. Cook the bacon in a large nonstick skillet over medium heat until crisp. Remove with a slotted spoon to the paper-lined plate. Pour off all but 1 tablespoon of the bacon fat.

In a bowl, beat the eggs, water, herbes de Provence, salt, and pepper until foamy and light. Return the pan to medium heat and add the eggs to the hot bacon fat. With a silicone spatula, push the eggs across the pan, scraping the cooked eggs off the bottom of the pan in large, fluffy curds that are tender and slightly moist. The eggs will take no more than 8 minutes. Do not let them brown or dry out; remember they will be baked again, inside the pie. Scrape the eggs into a medium bowl and fold in the bacon, cheese, and chives. Cool completely.

Line two baking sheets with parchment. Place a Baking Steel, baking stone, or inverted baking sheet on the center rack and heat the oven to 400°F.

Remove one block of dough from the refrigerator. Roll out the dough to an approximate 11-inch square, cut into 12 (3½- to 4½-inch) rectangles. Add a packed scant ¼ cup filling to one rectangle and form a hand pie with a second rectangle. Transfer to a baking sheet and firmly fork-crimp the edges. Vent with three short diagonal slashes across the top. Brush the surface with egg wash. (See Forming, Crimping, and Venting Hand Pies, page 30, for complete instructions.)

Continue to make and slash the remaining pies. Refrigerate or freeze while repeating the process with the other block of pie dough to make a total of 12 hand pies.

Bake the hand pies for 30 to 35 minutes, until deeply golden brown. I prefer to bake them one baking sheet at a time to take advantage of the Baking Steel in my oven. If you prefer to bake the two sheet pans at the same time, switch their position from top to bottom and front to back halfway through the bake.

Freeze hand pies (baked or unbaked) for up to 3 months (see Storing, Freezing, and Reheating, page 31).

SPINACH, CRANBERRY, PECAN, AND BLUE CHEESE HAND PIES

Makes 12

2 tablespoons (28 g) unsalted butter

¼ cup (28 g) diced shallots (about 2 medium)

8 ounces (225 g) frozen chopped spinach, defrosted and squeezed dry (about ½ cup)

¼ cup (42 g) dried cranberries

¼ cup (28 g) chopped candied pecans

4 tablespoons (2 ounces, 56 g) cream cheese, at room temperature, cubed

2 tablespoons chopped fresh flat-leaf parsley

½ cup (56 g) crumbled blue cheese

2 batches All-Butter Pie Dough, page 251, formed into square blocks

Egg wash (1 egg beaten with 1 tablespoon cool water and ¼ teaspoon kosher salt)

A welcome addition to the holiday buffet table, here is a satisfying vegetarian hand pie that is also ideal for picnics. It has a winning combination of spinach and candied nuts balanced by creamy, sharp blue cheese. I love the chew of dried cranberries in the filling, but golden raisins, dried tart cherries, or chopped dried mango are fine substitutions. The filling is sweet, green, textural, and salty and hits all my happy buttons.

Line two baking sheets with parchment. Place a Baking Steel, baking stone, or inverted baking sheet on the center rack and heat the oven to 400°F.

In a wide skillet, melt the butter over medium-high heat until foaming. Add the shallots and cook until wilted, then stir in the spinach and continue cooking and stirring over medium-high heat until the mixture is dry. Scrape into a medium bowl. Stir in the cranberries, pecans, softened cream cheese, and parsley. Cool completely. Fold in the blue cheese.

Remove one block of dough from the refrigerator. Roll out the dough to an approximate 11-inch square, cut into 12 (2½- to 3½-inch) rectangles, and vent half of them. Add a packed scant ¼ cup filling to one rectangle and form a hand pie with a second (vented) rectangle. Transfer to a baking sheet and firmly fork-crimp the edges. Brush the surface with egg wash. (See Forming, Crimping, and Venting Hand Pies, page 30, for complete instructions.)

Continue to make the remaining pies. Refrigerate or freeze while repeating the process with the other block of pie dough to make a total of 12 hand pies.

Bake the hand pies for 30 to 35 minutes, until deeply golden brown. I prefer to bake them one baking sheet at a time to take advantage of the Baking Steel in my oven. If you prefer to bake the two sheet pans at the same time, switch their position from top to bottom and front to back halfway through the bake.

Freeze hand pies (baked or unbaked) for up to 3 months (see Storing, Freezing, and Reheating, page 31).

BROCCOLI CHEDDAR HAND PIES

Makes 12

12 ounces (340 g) frozen broccoli florets

8 tablespoons (4 ounces, 113 g) cream cheese, cubed

½ teaspoon grated garlic

1 teaspoon kosher salt

½ teaspoon freshly ground black pepper

4 ounces (113 g) cheddar cheese, shredded

2 recipes Caramelized Onion and Cheese Pie Dough, page 259, formed into square blocks

Egg wash (1 egg beaten with 1 tablespoon cool water and ¼ teaspoon kosher salt)

When the afternoon hungries arrive, this familiar combination hits the spot. My friend Ally rhapsodized with such passion about her after-school snacking on broccoli and cheese pastries, I immediately added the combination to this book. Savory, satisfying, and vegetarian, they can be baked straight from the freezer, even in a kid-friendly toaster oven. I use frozen broccoli because it's so much easier to chop into smaller pieces and still retain form. Swap in cauliflower if you're not a broccoli fan. Replace some of the broccoli with shredded chicken, if you wish.

Line two baking sheets with parchment. Place a Baking Steel, baking stone, or inverted baking sheet on the center rack and heat the oven to 400°F.

Let the broccoli warm on the counter for about 5 minutes. Then, with a chef's knife, chop the pieces so each is no larger than an almond. With a sturdy spoon in a wide bowl, beat the cream cheese, garlic, salt, and pepper until thoroughly combined. Fold in the chopped broccoli and shredded cheese until everything is coated. I use my hands for this.

Remove one block of dough from the refrigerator. Roll out the dough to an approximate 11-inch square, cut into 12 (2½- to 3½-inch) rectangles, and vent half of them. Add a packed scant ¼ cup filling to one rectangle and form a hand pie with a second (vented) rectangle. Transfer to a baking sheet and firmly fork-crimp the edges. Brush the surface with egg wash. (See Forming, Crimping, and Venting Hand Pies, page 30, for complete instructions.)

(Continued)

Continue to make the remaining pies. Refrigerate or freeze while repeating the process with the other block of pie dough to make a total of 12 hand pies.

Bake the hand pies for 30 to 35 minutes, until deeply golden brown. I prefer to bake them one baking sheet at a time to take advantage of the Baking Steel in my oven. If you prefer to bake the two sheet pans at the same time, switch their position from top to bottom and front to back halfway through the bake.

Freeze hand pies (baked or unbaked) for up to 3 months (see Storing, Freezing, and Reheating, page 31).

SESAME CHICKEN HAND PIES

Makes 12

1½ tablespoons toasted sesame oil

1 tablespoon orange juice

1 tablespoon tamari or low-sodium soy sauce

1 tablespoon cornstarch

2 teaspoons grated fresh ginger

1 garlic clove, slivered

½ to ¾ teaspoon crushed red pepper flakes

½ teaspoon kosher salt

½ pound (225 g) boneless chicken thighs, cut into bite-sized cubes

2 tablespoons grapeseed or canola oil

½ cup (70 g) ½-inch diced carrot (about 1 large)

¼ cup (25 g) thinly sliced scallions (about 2)

½ cup (70 g) frozen peas

2 tablespoons sherry

¼ cup (30 g) salted peanuts, chopped

1 tablespoon chopped cilantro leaves

1 tablespoon lime juice

---

2 recipes Cream Cheese Pie Dough, page 252, formed into square blocks

Egg wash (1 egg beaten with 1 tablespoon cool water and ¼ teaspoon kosher salt)

About 2 or 3 tablespoons toasted sesame seeds

With the zing of chili, the crunch of peanuts, and a toasty sesame-scented filling, everybody's take-out favorite becomes a pie. The peas and carrots offer color, and the ginger wakes up the taste buds for a crowd favorite. Omit the peanuts if there are allergy concerns; instead, add pepitas or slivered almonds for some crunch. I like a spicy mix, so I opt for the full amount of red pepper flakes—adjust the zing to fit your own tastes, using the lesser amount if unsure. Serve with a shredded cabbage slaw dressed with rice wine vinegar and sesame oil. Make sure to use a nonstick skillet or you will hate me when you do the dishes.

Line two baking sheets with parchment.

Whisk the sesame oil, orange juice, tamari, cornstarch, ginger, garlic, red pepper flakes, and salt together. Stir in the cubed chicken and coat well with the marinade. Cover and refrigerate for at least 1 hour, or up to 1 day.

In a wide, large, nonstick skillet, warm the oil over a medium-high heat. Add the carrot and scallions and cook until just wilted, about 3 minutes. Spoon the chicken and marinade into the pan carefully; it's likely to spatter. Increase the heat to high and stir-fry quickly, until the chicken is browned in places and cooked through and the sauce has thickened, 6 to 8 minutes.

Add the peas and sherry and bring to a boil. Let the mixture bubble and boil for 1 minute, until the sauce is thick and coating the chicken. Stir in the peanuts, cilantro, and lime juice. Cool the filling completely before proceeding, about 30 minutes. Place a Baking Steel, baking stone, or inverted baking sheet on the center rack and heat the oven to 400°F.

Remove one block of dough from the refrigerator. Roll out the dough to an approximate 11-inch square, cut into

12 (2½- to 3½-inch) rectangles, and vent half of them. Add a packed scant ¼ cup filling to one rectangle and form a hand pie with a second (vented) rectangle. Transfer to a baking sheet and firmly fork-crimp the edges. Brush the surface with egg wash. (See Forming, Crimping, and Venting Hand Pies, page 30, for complete instructions.) Scatter the sesame seeds across the surface.

Continue to make the remaining pies. Refrigerate or freeze while repeating the process with the other block of pie dough to make a total of 12 hand pies.

Bake the hand pies for 30 to 35 minutes, until deeply golden brown. I prefer to bake them one baking sheet at a time to take advantage of the Baking Steel in my oven. If you want to bake them at the same time, switch them top to bottom and front to back halfway through the bake.

Freeze hand pies (baked or unbaked) for up to 3 months (see Storing, Freezing, and Reheating, page 31).

CHEESEBURGER HAND PIES

Makes 12

---

2 slices
(2 ounces, 56 g)
thick-cut smoked
bacon, diced

1 tablespoon
minced shallot

¼ teaspoon
minced garlic

½ pound (225 g)
ground beef (80
percent lean)

1 tablespoon
tomato paste

¼ teaspoon
kosher salt

¼ teaspoon
freshly ground
black pepper

2 tablespoons
mayonnaise

2 tablespoons
ketchup

½ cup (56 g)
shredded sharp
cheddar cheese

---

2 recipes
Everything Spice
Pie Dough, page
257, formed into
square blocks

About 10 dill
pickle slices
(coins), optional

Egg white wash
(1 egg white,
lightly beaten
with ¼ **teaspoon**
kosher salt)

About 2 or 3
tablespoons
toasted sesame
seeds

With special sauce, a pickle slice, and sesame seeds scattered on the top of this round hand pie, expect to hear, "It tastes just like a cheeseburger!" The everything crust is a logical choice, adding an extra boost of onion and garlic flavor and a speckled exterior, but I love them just as much with the caramelized onion and cheese crust. Perfect for game day, a picnic, or an after-school treat.

Line a dinner plate with paper towels. In a small skillet, cook the bacon over medium heat until crisp. Use a slotted spoon to remove the crisped bacon to the plate to cool. Pour off all but 1 tablespoon of the bacon fat. Add the shallot and garlic to the pan and stir and cook over medium heat until wilted and beginning to brown, just a minute or so. Scrape out the shallots and garlic into a mixing bowl.

Add the ground beef to the skillet and, using two wooden spoons, break up the meat until it is crumbly and just cooked through with no red remaining. Stir in the tomato paste, cook until combined, and add the salt and pepper. Add the meat mixture and the bacon into the mixing bowl with the shallot and garlic, and stir.

Spread the filling out on a baking sheet, cover, and refrigerate to chill it for about 20 minutes. If making well ahead, cover the bowl, and refrigerate.

In a small bowl, combine the mayonnaise and ketchup. Stir the cheese into the cold meat filling.

Line two baking sheets with parchment. Place a Baking Steel, baking stone, or inverted baking sheet on the center rack and heat the oven to 400°F.

Remove one block of dough from the refrigerator. Roll out the dough to an approximate 11-inch square, cut out 12 (3½-inch) rounds, and vent half of them. Form a "cheeseburger" with a swipe of the mayonnaise mixture on one round, topped with a slice of pickle, then the meat and cheese filling. Top with a second (vented) round to form a hand pie. Transfer to a baking sheet and firmly fork-crimp the edges. (See Forming, Crimping, and Venting Hand Pies, page 30, for complete instructions.)

Repeat the process to make five more pies. Brush the surface of each with the egg white wash and sprinkle with sesame seeds. Refrigerate or freeze while repeating the process with the other block of pie dough to make a total of 12 hand pies.

Bake for 25 to 30 minutes, until deeply golden brown. I prefer to bake them one baking sheet at a time to take advantage of the Baking Steel in my oven. If you prefer to bake the two sheet pans at the same time, switch their position from top to bottom and front to back halfway through the bake.

Freeze hand pies (baked or unbaked) for up to 3 months (see Storing, Freezing, and Reheating, page 31).

KALBI SHORT RIB HAND PIES

Makes 12

½ cup (120 ml) sesame oil

¼ cup (60 ml) tamari or low-sodium soy sauce

¼ cup (60 ml) mirin (rice wine)

¼ cup (60 ml) rice wine vinegar

¼ cup (53 g) packed brown sugar

1 tablespoon grated garlic

1 tablespoon grated fresh ginger

1½ pounds (680 g) flanken or kalbi-style short ribs (¾ inch thick)

½ cup (50 g) chopped scallions (about 4)

2 tablespoons gochujang paste

2 tablespoons chopped cilantro leaves

2 recipes All-Butter Pie Dough, page 251, formed into square blocks

Egg white wash (1 egg white, lightly beaten with ¼ teaspoon kosher salt)

Short ribs are deeply flavorful, but because the meat is muscled, it takes low and slow heat to become fall-apart tender. While long-cooked braises have their place, there's another short rib recipe that is quick and delicious, flavorful and chewy (in a good way): Korean-style kalbi short ribs are marinated in a spicy brew and then grilled or broiled hot and fast. The recipe requires a different cut of short rib, called either kalbi or flanken cut, available at many Asian markets and on order from a butcher. In this cut, the butcher slices across, not between, the ribs, for long, slim meaty pieces, each with four small bones. Once cooked, cut away the bones (Korean chefs use scissors) and chop the meat. That's the way to turn short ribs into a special occasion hand pie, rich and satisfying.

Combine the sesame oil, tamari, mirin, vinegar, brown sugar, garlic, and ginger in a medium bowl. Place the short ribs in a shallow glass or ceramic baking dish and pour the marinade over the meat. Cover and refrigerate for at least 4 hours, or as long as overnight. Turn the short ribs a few times now and again, if you remember.

Fire up the grill and get it screaming hot. Place the ribs on the grill (reserve the marinade) and do not look away. Turn them over in 3 or 4 minutes and grill the other side for 3 or 4 minutes longer. They should have blackened tips and edges, bubbling fat, and smell delicious. That's all it takes. The meat will be medium-rare.

Alternatively, to broil: Place a rack in the uppermost part of the oven (and turn on the fan; this will make some smoke). Line a baking sheet with a snug covering of foil. Place the short ribs in a single layer on the lined pan and reserve the marinade. Broil for

(Continued)

4 to 6 minutes per side until the meat is blackened on the edges, the fat is sizzling, and the scent is very appetizing.

Let the ribs cool for a few minutes, then remove the bones using a sharp knife or kitchen scissors. Place the meat on a cutting board and chop into bite-sized pieces. Leave some of the fat to keep the filling moist, but remove any gristle.

Pour the marinade into a small saucepan and bring to a boil over high heat. Cook until thickened and reduced by half, to about ⅔ to ¾ cup (150 to 180 ml) sticky sauce, about 10 minutes. Be careful in the last moments as it can scorch. Combine the meat and half of the sauce, to start. The filling should be somewhat saucy, but still easy to scoop, so add more sauce if needed. Do not over-sauce! (Leftover sauce can be swiped on a sandwich.) Cover and cool completely, during which time the filling will firm up slightly.

Place a Baking Steel, baking stone, or inverted baking sheet on the center rack and heat the oven to 400°F. Line two baking sheets with parchment. Stir the scallions, gochujang, and cilantro into the filling.

Remove one block of dough from the refrigerator. Roll out the dough to an approximate 11-inch square, cut into 12 (2½- to 3½-inch) rectangles, and vent half of them. Add a packed scant ¼ cup filling to one rectangle and form a hand pie with a second (vented) rectangle. Transfer to a baking sheet and firmly fork-crimp the edges. Brush the surface with the egg white wash. (See Forming, Crimping, and Venting Hand Pies, page 30, for complete instructions.)

Continue to make the remaining pies. Refrigerate or freeze while repeating the process with the other block of pie dough to make a total of 12 hand pies.

Bake the hand pies for 30 to 35 minutes, until deeply golden brown. I prefer to bake them one baking sheet at a time to take advantage of the Baking Steel in my oven. If you prefer to bake the two sheet pans at the same time, switch their position from top to bottom and front to back halfway through the bake.

Freeze hand pies (baked or unbaked) for up to 3 months (see Storing, Freezing, and Reheating, page 31).

LAMB ROGAN JOSH HAND PIES

Makes 12

1 tablespoon grapeseed or canola oil

½ pound (225 g) ground lamb

½ cup (70 g) diced onion

1 cup (225 g) canned crushed tomatoes

1½ teaspoons minced fresh ginger

1 teaspoon minced garlic

1 teaspoon curry powder

½ teaspoon kosher salt

¼ teaspoon turmeric

⅛ teaspoon cayenne pepper

½ Turkish or California bay leaf (or 1 Indian bay leaf)

½ cup (70 g) frozen peas

2 tablespoons plain full-fat yogurt

¼ cup (15 g) cilantro, chopped

¼ teaspoon garam masala

2 recipes All-Butter Pie Dough, page 251, formed into square blocks

Egg wash (1 egg beaten with 1 tablespoon cool water and ¼ teaspoon kosher salt)

Cilantro Chutney (recipe follows), optional

Rogan josh, that quintessential dish served at great and terrible Indian restaurants around the world, makes the most of the singular flavor of lamb in a tomato gravy lightened with yogurt, a dash of curry, and the slightly sweet overtones of garam masala. If you can find bay leaves from India, it's worth using one here. They're more lightly flavored and less assertive. If not, use only half a Turkish or California bay leaf, either dry or fresh. Serve the pies with any chutney, but I like to make a batch of cilantro chutney for the balance it adds—herbal with chile heat that plays nicely with the warmth of the curry.

Heat the oil in a large skillet over medium-high heat until shimmering. Add the lamb and break the meat apart while cooking until all the pink is gone. Using a slotted spoon, lift the lamb out of the pan into a medium bowl. Pour off all but 1 tablespoon of the fat in the skillet, if necessary.

Add the onions to the pan and cook over medium to medium-high heat until they are turning deep brown on the edges, but not blackening, about 12 minutes. Stir in the crushed tomatoes, ginger, garlic, curry powder, salt, turmeric, cayenne, and bay leaf. Bring to a boil, then reduce the heat to medium-low and cook gently for 20 minutes, until thickened and reduced by half. Remove and discard the bay leaf. Add the tomato mixture to the lamb and stir well. Stir in the peas, yogurt, cilantro, and garam masala. Cover and refrigerate until cold, at least 1 hour. (To speed the process, spread the mixture across a baking sheet and refrigerate or freeze. It will be cold in 20 minutes or so.)

(Continued)

Line a baking sheet with parchment. Place a Baking Steel, baking stone, or inverted baking sheet on the center rack and heat the oven to 400°F.

Remove one block of dough from the refrigerator. Roll out the dough to an approximate 11-inch square, cut into 12 (2½- to 3½-inch) rectangles, and vent half of them. Add a packed scant ¼ cup filling to one rectangle and form a hand pie with a second (vented) rectangle. Transfer to a baking sheet and firmly fork-crimp the edges. Brush the surface with egg wash. (See Forming, Crimping, and Venting Hand Pies, page 30, for complete instructions.)

Continue to make the remaining pies. Refrigerate while repeating the process with the other block of pie dough to make a total of 12 hand pies.

Bake the hand pies for 30 to 35 minutes, until deeply golden brown. I prefer to bake them one baking sheet at a time to take advantage of the Baking Steel in my oven. If you prefer to bake the two sheet pans at the same time, switch their position from top to bottom and front to back halfway through the bake.

Serve with the cilantro chutney if you like.

Freeze hand pies (baked or unbaked) for up to 3 months (see Storing, Freezing, and Reheating, page 31).

CILANTRO CHUTNEY

Makes about ½ cup

1 cup (60 g) cilantro leaves and stems

½ cup (30 g) mint leaves

¼ teaspoon sugar

⅛ teaspoon ground cumin

¼ to ½ teaspoon minced seeded Thai bird chile

¼ to ⅓ cup (60 to 80 ml) freshly squeezed lime juice

Serve the Lamb Rogan Josh Hand Pies with this bright cilantro chutney. Any leftover chutney matches with the Samosa Cigars (page 201), or may be served with sharp cheese, or spooned over scrambled eggs. Use as much minced chile as your crowd will tolerate.

Use a mini chopper, food processor, or (my preference) a chef's knife to chop the cilantro, mint, sugar, ground cumin, and chile together until the herbs are chopped fine. This might take some work if chopping by hand. Scrape the chopped herbs into a bowl, then add ¼ cup lime juice and stir together until blended and thick. Add more lime juice if needed to make a thick saucy condiment. Chill the chutney at least 1 hour to let the flavor develop. Keep refrigerated. This chutney will not last more than a day before turning an unappetizing color.

BET-YOU-A-BLUEBERRY FROSTED HAND PIES

Makes 12

2/3 cup (135 g) granulated sugar

1/4 cup (28 g) cornstarch

4 teaspoons lemon juice

3 cups (460 g) blueberries, picked over and washed

3/4 teaspoon ground cinnamon

1/4 teaspoon freshly grated nutmeg

2 recipes All-Butter Pie Dough, page 251, formed into square blocks

Egg wash (1 egg beaten with 1 tablespoon cool water and 1/4 teaspoon kosher salt)

2 tablespoons cold milk

1/2 teaspoon vanilla extract

2 cups (225 g) powdered sugar

Rainbow sprinkles

I have such sweet memories of my Grandfather Allan. He told tall tales of swinging on vines with Tarzan, diving in the oceans to find Atlantis, and catching barehanded a lobster with claws as big as his head. I loved him dearly. One of my most treasured possessions is a letter he sent two-year-old me with reassurances that a baby brother was not, as I feared, the end of the world. In fact, he bet me a blueberry I would come to love my brother, and indeed, I did. I'll bet you a blueberry you'll love these little pies.

In a large heavy pot, stir together the sugar, cornstarch, and lemon juice. Add the blueberries and turn the heat to medium-high. With a potato masher, crush about half of the blueberries to form a loose fruity stew, stirring continually so it will not stick. Bring the mixture to a boil and cook for exactly 1 minute, until thickened. Stir in the cinnamon and nutmeg and set aside to cool completely before making the hand pies; it will thicken further as it cools. The filling may be made up to 5 days in advance.

Line two baking sheets with parchment. Place a Baking Steel, baking stone, or inverted baking sheet on the center rack and heat the oven to 400°F.

Remove one block of dough from the refrigerator. Roll out the dough to an approximate 11-inch square, cut into 12 (2½- to 3½-inch) rectangles, and vent half of them. Add a packed scant ¼ cup filling to one rectangle and form a hand pie with a second (vented) rectangle. Transfer to a baking sheet and firmly fork-crimp the edges. Brush the surface with egg wash. (See Forming, Crimping, and Venting Hand Pies, page 30, for complete instructions.)

(Continued)

Continue to make the remaining pies. Refrigerate or freeze while repeating the process with the other block of pie dough to make a total of 12 hand pies.

Bake the hand pies for 30 to 35 minutes, until deeply golden brown. I prefer to bake them one baking sheet at a time to take advantage of the Baking Steel in my oven. If you prefer to bake the two sheet pans at the same time, switch their position from top to bottom and front to back halfway through the bake.

Freeze unfrosted hand pies (baked or unbaked) for up to 3 months (see Storing, Freezing, and Reheating, page 31).

Whisk the milk and vanilla together and then whisk into the powdered sugar until smooth and very thick. If it isn't coming together, dribble in the tiniest additional amount of milk. If it's too thin, add more powdered sugar. Transfer to a pastry bag or ziptop bag, snip off a corner, and squiggle the frosting across the surface of each pie. (Or use an offset spatula to spread the frosting evenly across the surface, inside the crimped edges.) Garnish enthusiastically with plenty of rainbow sprinkles. Let the frosting set up, about 30 minutes, before serving.

BROWN SUGAR–CINNAMON HAND PIES

Makes 12

---

2 cups (426 g) packed dark brown sugar

⅓ cup (40 g) all-purpose flour

1½ tablespoons cocoa powder (Dutch process or natural, it doesn't matter)

3 tablespoons ground cinnamon

½ teaspoon freshly grated nutmeg

¼ teaspoon kosher salt

4 tablespoons (56 g) unsalted butter, melted

---

2 recipes All-Butter Pie Dough, page 251, formed into square blocks

Egg wash (1 egg beaten with 1 tablespoon cool water and ¼ teaspoon kosher salt)

---

2 tablespoons cold milk

½ teaspoon vanilla extract

2 cups (225 g) powdered sugar

Sparkling sugar

There's a certain popular brown sugar breakfast pastry that was my constant companion through years of riding horses and hot days at competitions. I kept packets in the trunk of my car for plummeting blood sugar moments, but also because they were a food filled with memories, a childhood favorite with a slightly sandy filling offset by sugary, silky frosting. Using common pantry ingredients, these pies retain those familiar qualities, but so much more deliciously. Adding cocoa powder will not make the filling taste like chocolate at all, but only serves to intensify the spicy cinnamon—a trick I picked up from Maida Heatter's cinnamon swirl bread.

Line two baking sheets with parchment. Place a Baking Steel, baking stone, or inverted baking sheet on the center rack and heat the oven to 400°F.

Stir the brown sugar, flour, cocoa powder, cinnamon, nutmeg, and salt together. Add the melted butter and stir until the filling is thick and no longer powdery at all.

Remove one block of dough from the refrigerator. Roll out the dough to an approximate 11-inch square, cut into 12 (2½- to 3½-inch) rectangles, and vent half of them. Add a packed scant ¼ cup filling to one rectangle and form a hand pie with a second (vented) rectangle. Transfer to a baking sheet and firmly fork-crimp the edges. Brush the surface with egg wash. (See Forming, Crimping, and Venting Hand Pies, page 30, for complete instructions.)

Continue to make the remaining pies. Refrigerate or freeze while repeating the process with the other block of pie dough to make a total of 12 hand pies.

(Continued)

Bake the hand pies for 30 to 35 minutes, until deeply golden brown. I prefer to bake them one baking sheet at a time to take advantage of the Baking Steel in my oven. If you prefer to bake the two sheet pans at the same time, switch their position from top to bottom and front to back halfway through the bake.

Freeze unfrosted hand pies (baked or unbaked) for up to 3 months (see Storing, Freezing, and Reheating, page 31).

Whisk the milk and vanilla together and then whisk into the powdered sugar until smooth and very thick. If it isn't coming together, dribble in the tiniest additional amount of milk. If it's too thin, add more powdered sugar. Transfer to a pastry bag or ziptop bag, snip off a corner, and squiggle the frosting across the surface of each pie. (Or use an offset spatula to spread the frosting evenly across the surface, inside the crimped edges.) Garnish enthusiastically with plenty of sparkling sugar. Let the frosting set up, about 30 minutes, before serving.

MOCHA CREAM HAND PIES

Makes 12

2 recipes Chocolate Pie Dough, page 256, formed into square blocks

Coffee Pastry Cream (recipe follows)

Egg wash (1 egg beaten with 1 tablespoon cool water and ¼ teaspoon kosher salt)

2 tablespoons ice cold coffee

2 cups (225 g) powdered sugar

Chocolate sprinkles

As a child I would wait all year for a trip to the Sullivan Square mothership of all things ice cream: Schrafft's. My Bostonian grandmother, Bea, and I would share a dish of ice cream with jimmies (New Englanders' chocolate sprinkles). It was deliciously decadent. Bea loved coffee ice cream and because I worshipped her, so did I, so we each dipped our spoon into the creamy goodness served in a footed stainless-steel bowl. My admiration for coffee ice cream has never diminished and this is my love letter to Schrafft's coffee ice cream, with jimmies. I'm not going to lie. The chocolate pie dough is challenging and making these hand pies is a bit of a project, but your reward is in the final product: a very, very grown-up pastry.

Line two baking sheets with parchment. Place a Baking Steel, baking stone, or inverted baking sheet on the center rack and heat the oven to 400°F.

Remove one block of dough from the refrigerator. Roll out the dough to an approximate 11-inch square, cut into 12 (2½- to 3½-inch) rectangles, and vent half of them. Add a packed scant ¼ cup pastry cream to one rectangle and form a hand pie with a second (vented) rectangle. Transfer to a baking sheet and firmly fork-crimp the edges. Brush the surface with egg wash. (See Forming, Crimping, and Venting Hand Pies, page 30, for complete instructions.)

Continue to make the remaining pies. Refrigerate or freeze while repeating the process with the other block of pie dough to make a total of 12 hand pies.

Bake the hand pies for 30 to 35 minutes, until firm to the touch. I prefer to bake them one baking sheet at a time to take advantage of the Baking Steel in my oven. If you prefer to bake the two sheet pans at the same time, switch their position from top to bottom and front to back halfway through the bake.

Whisk the coffee into the powdered sugar until smooth and very thick. If it isn't coming together, dribble in the tiniest additional amount of coffee. If it's too thin, add more powdered sugar. Use an offset spatula to spread the frosting evenly across the surface, inside the crimped edges. Garnish enthusiastically with plenty of chocolate sprinkles. Let the frosting set up, about 30 minutes, before serving.

These hand pies will not freeze well. Keep them, well wrapped and refrigerated, for no more than 2 days. Best enjoyed cold.

COFFEE PASTRY CREAM

Makes 3 cups (750 g)

3 cups (720 ml) whole milk

1½ cups (115 g) whole coffee beans

¾ cup (150 g) granulated sugar

¼ teaspoon kosher salt

6 tablespoons cornstarch

2 tablespoons all-purpose flour

6 large egg yolks

½ teaspoon vanilla extract

4 tablespoons (56 g) unsalted butter

Pastry cream gets buzzed with this variation on the classic recipe. If you're sensitive to caffeine, use decaf beans.

Combine 2½ cups of the milk, the coffee beans, sugar, and salt in a medium saucepan over medium-high heat. Let the mixture warm, stirring all the time as the sugar dissolves, about 4 minutes. Cover, remove from the heat, and steep for at least 1 hour, or up to 3 hours. Pass the coffee milk through a strainer to remove and discard the coffee beans. Set the coffee milk aside.

Set a strainer over a bowl placed inside an ice bath. In a small mixing bowl, whisk the remaining ½ cup milk with the cornstarch, flour, and egg yolks.

Return the coffee milk to the stove and reheat until tiny bubbles form around the edges of the pan, just 2 or 3 minutes. Slowly whisk ½ cup of the hot coffee milk mixture into the egg yolk mixture. This is called tempering and will keep the yolks from scrambling. Pour the egg/milk mixture back into the warm milk, whisking the whole time. Return the pan to medium-high heat and bring the mixture to a boil, constantly whisking, until the mixture thickens into a smooth sauce. This will happen very suddenly, so stay vigilant. The coffee cream will be thick like warm pudding in about 5 minutes.

Remove the pan from the heat and use the whisk or a sturdy spoon to push the custard through the strainer into the bowl over the ice bath to remove any lumps. Stir in the vanilla and butter.

Cover with plastic wrap touching the surface of the custard to keep a skin from forming. Refrigerate for 2 hours, or until entirely cool. The custard will keep 3 days, but it's best when fresh. Custard does not freeze well.

LEMON MERINGUE TARTLETTES

Makes 12

---

2 recipes Cream Cheese Pie Dough, page 252, shaped into 3- by 4-inch rectangular blocks

Egg wash (1 egg beaten with 1 tablespoon cool water and ¼ teaspoon kosher salt)

3 egg whites (90 g), at room temperature

¼ teaspoon cream of tartar

½ cup (100 g) granulated sugar

¼ teaspoon vanilla extract

2½ cups (680 g) Lemon Curd (recipe follows) or store-bought

Lemon meringue pie is a classic. When I serve these personal LMPs, pretty as a picture sitting on the sideboard before lunch, I see guests' eyes rove to the bright, cloud-like tops before the first course is served. Remarkably easy to put together, I'm so enamored of these tartlettes that I keep lemon curd in the freezer, along with ziptop bags of egg whites (they'll keep for 6 months) left over from custard and ice cream making. Develop a reputation for lemon tartlettes at the drop of a hat.

Heat the oven to 375°F. Line two baking sheets with parchment. Roll one dough block out to an approximate 9- by 14-inch rectangle. Use a 4½-inch cookie cutter (or a small plate) to cut out 6 rounds of dough. Move each round to the baking sheet and roll the edge inward, pinching and crimping to make a tart shell. Use a fork to prick holes (or "dock") the centers and brush the edge with egg wash. Place the baking sheet in the freezer and repeat with the other dough block. Chill the 12 tart shells hard in the freezer for 30 minutes.

Drape a small piece of foil over each tart shell. Fill the foil with pie weights and blind bake (see page 100) the shells for 20 minutes. Remove the foil and weights and continue to bake an additional 10 minutes to dry out the crusts. Remove and cool on a rack.

In the bowl of a stand mixer with the whisk attachment, beat the egg whites on high until they are good and foamy. Add the cream of tartar and continue to beat on high. When the whites turn opaque, begin to add the sugar slowly, 1 tablespoon at a time, while the mixer continues to run. Once all the sugar has been incorporated, add the vanilla and beat until fully incorporated. Stop the mixer and lift the beater: You're looking for a stiff peak, a very lofty meringue that stands up on its own. It will be glossy and smooth and sturdy. Be careful not to overbeat—the meringue should be shiny and moist, not dry.

Now you're ready to put together the tartlettes. Place an oven rack about 6 inches from the top of the oven, close to the broiler element. Keep in mind the meringue will top the crust and be quite tall, as much as 2 inches above the baking sheet. In my oven, that means I place the rack in the top position. Turn the oven to broil.

Spoon 3 generous tablespoons of lemon curd into each crust, avoiding the edges. It should be thick and piled on. Add the meringue either by piping it or scooping up a big spoonful and plopping it across the surface, using the back of the spoon to make fluffy clouds. Here is a chance to decorate with a flourish, especially if you have a pastry bag and know how to use a St. Honoré tip.

Pop the tartlettes under the broiler for 3 or 4 minutes—not long at all. Do not take your eyes off the oven and open the door to peek frequently. Broil until you smell the unmistakable scent of toasting marshmallows. Let the edges and tips get very, very, slightly blackened like a campfire marshmallow. Now, they're ready.

Serve within a few hours.

LEMON CURD

Makes 3 cups (750 g)

4 large eggs, plus
4 large egg yolks

1 cup (200 g)
granulated sugar

1 tablespoon
finely grated zest
and ⅔ cup (160 ml)
juice from 4 ripe,
juicy lemons

¼ teaspoon
kosher salt

4 tablespoons
(56 g) unsalted
butter, cubed

This will make more than you need for the tartlettes. But it's no hardship to find a way to use the glorious, velvety, tart, and sunny yellow custard. Scones are a happy place for lemon curd. So is a spoon. I can barely keep this in the house, I'm so wild for lemon curd. For a lemony, floral, sweet curd, search out Meyer lemons, widely available in grocery stores in late winter and early spring. That's when I make extra batches of curd and freeze them in pint-sized containers.

Fill a medium saucepan with 2 inches of water and heat over medium heat until barely bubbling. Whisk the eggs, egg yolks, and sugar in a heatproof bowl that will fit over the pot without touching the water below. Set the bowl over the simmering water and whisk constantly until the mixture thickens, becomes pale, and forms a ribbon when the whisk is pulled out of it. Use a thermometer for precision—the curd should be 140°F.

Remove the bowl from the pot and stir the zest, juice, and salt into the curd. The custard will be thin, so return the bowl to the pot over the simmering water and stir over medium heat as the mixture thickens. Continue cooking, watching the temperature: It's done when it reaches 170°F, or when a finger run across the back of a coated spoon leaves a trail.

For a velvety texture, press the custard through a fine-mesh strainer to remove any flecks of zest or egg. Whisk in the butter, one cube at a time, and watch the curd turn shiny and thick.

Cool, cover, and refrigerate for 4 or more hours. Curd can be frozen for 6 months.

OLD-FASHIONED APPLE DUMPLINGS

Makes 4

⅓ cup (3 g) pecans, toasted and chopped

4 tablespoons (56 g) unsalted butter, at room temperature

¼ cup (53 g) packed brown sugar

½ teaspoon grated orange zest

¼ teaspoon ground cinnamon

⅛ teaspoon freshly grated nutmeg

4 firm tart apples

1 recipe Cream Cheese Pie Dough, page 252, formed into a square block

Egg wash (1 egg beaten with 1 tablespoon cool water and ¼ teaspoon kosher salt)

Sparkling sugar

Warm Caramel Sauce (recipe follows), optional

In the fall, an easy dessert is a baked apple filled with nuts and spices served with cold cream poured over the still warm apple. An apple dumpling is all that, plus pie dough. It's a beautiful dessert from the most basic ingredients. Stuffed with nuts and spices, wrapped in flaky dough, and covered in a thick coating of sparkling sugar, here is a personal apple pie on a plate, pretty as a picture. Use a firm tart pie apple, no larger than 3 inches in diameter, something crisp that will soften in the oven but not turn mushy.

Adjust the oven rack to the center. Place a Baking Steel, baking stone, or inverted baking sheet on the center rack and heat the oven to 400°F. Line a baking sheet with parchment and spray lightly with nonstick cooking spray.

Stir together the pecans, butter, brown sugar, orange zest, cinnamon, and nutmeg. Peel each apple, then remove the core and seeds from the top and the bottom so there is a tunnel through the center. This can be accomplished with a melon scoop, sharp grapefruit spoon, or small apple corer. Apples rarely sit up squarely, so trim a slim slice from the bottom of each to get them to sit flat. Fill the empty space in the core with the pecan mixture.

Divide the cream cheese dough into 4 pieces, each about 3 ounces (85 g). One at a time, on a flour dusted surface, roll each piece into a round that is about 6 inches in diameter (this size will depend on the size of the apple).

Place one filled apple in the center of one dough round and lift the edges to enclose the apple. Allow the dough to naturally pleat around the top of the apple. Pinch it together

(Continued)

at the top, trimming away the excess with sharp scissors. Repeat with the remaining apples and dough. Reroll the extra dough to cut out leaves and form 4 little round nubbins for stems. Using egg wash, attach two or three leaves and a stem to the top of each dumpling so it resembles an apple.

Place the sparkling sugar on a dinner plate. Paint each dough-covered apple on the sides and top (not the bottom) with the egg wash, then roll in the sugar to generously cover. Freeze the dumplings for 30 minutes.

Bake the dumplings for 35 to 45 minutes, depending on the size of the apple, until the dough is toasty brown and the juices from the apple are bubbling. Because the weight of the apple can make the base separate from the rest of the pastry, use a broad offset spatula to gently lift the dumpling to a plate. Serve warm.

To get fancy, plate the apples on pools of caramel sauce. A little ice cream and we're happy campers.

WARM CARAMEL SAUCE

Makes 1 cup

½ cup (120 ml) heavy cream

¼ cup (114 g) sour cream

1 cup (200 g) granulated sugar

¼ cup (60 ml) water

2 tablespoons light corn syrup

Whisk together the cream and sour cream in a small saucepan and warm gently over low heat.

In another saucepan, combine the sugar, water, and corn syrup. Boil, without stirring, until the mixture turns a medium amber, 8 to 10 minutes.

Remove the pan from the heat and whisk in the warm cream mixture. Set it aside for about 5 minutes, during which time the caramel will thicken. Transfer to a serving dish, boat, or pitcher. Or puddle on plates under the warm apple dumplings.

CHAPTER 3

PIE POPPERS

SNACKING PIES

Tiny pies for pass-around appetizers, picnic fare, airplane snack, or dessert for the buffet table, pie poppers are two-bite beauties that thrill with bold flavors and plenty of texture. Freeze unbaked pie poppers and rely on the toaster oven to feed drop-in visitors, hungry teens, or a late-night craving for an ice cream accompaniment.

When I first thought about flying pies, pies that are self-contained, I wanted nothing more than a miniature, teeny tiny pie—my dream come true. As much as I love pie and adore pie crust, there are times when I don't want an entire slice of pie, or even an entire hand pie: I only want a nibble, a bite, a satisfying, crusty, delicious tiny pie. Something to have with my coffee, to get me through the 3:30 p.m. hungries, to snack on late at night after a party. Pie poppers were born. Yes, I admit, they are fussy little fellows and take some time to form and crimp, but like any kitchen skill, you improve with practice. Each recipe yields 2 dozen tiny pies, enough to stash some away for a rainy day.

SIZE AND SHAPE: AVOIDING DOUGH WASTE

Dough waste is real. Any shape other than square or rectangular means dough is going to be thrown away. But here we are, making these cute little pies called poppers that beg to be round. So, I've done the math and figured out the best shape to roll the dough in order to cut out the most top and bottom crusts (because rerolling makes for tough crust, no flake, and difficult handling). But keep in mind, the dough should never be rolled any thinner than ⅛ inch, or it will be difficult to handle. (The pie dough recipes may be found on pages 251 to 259.)

To make matters more challenging, cookie cutters are inconsistently sized. I can call for a 2½-inch cutter in the recipe, and if your cutter is 2¾ inches, you will get fewer tiny pies. This is a huge frustration for a recipe writer who wants everything to work out perfectly for everyone every single time.

Here's how I plan: I sketch out my intentions, measuring the size of my cookie cutter (or biscuit cutter or a small drinking glass) and determine what size to roll the dough, and how many poppers I can expect from the sheet of dough. When I stamp out the rounds, I keep the cuts very close together to avoid wasting dough.

DAZZLING FILLINGS

Because poppers are two-bite wonders, the filling must not be shy. Bold, textural, and well-spiced will play well with the rich dough. Adding an ingredient like cranberries, kimchi, chopped nuts, or thinly sliced scallions makes a big difference to the flavor and texture of your filling, with no possibility for any one-note combination. The filling has to be chopped fine, too, so this means more work than a galette or a hand pie. But a popper serves a different purpose: It is snackable pie.

FORMING, CRIMPING, AND VENTING PIE POPPERS

Flour the surface generously and roll one block of dough to 9 by 13 inches, about ¼ inch thick. Use a round cookie cutter about 2 inches across to make 24 rounds, as close together as possible.

A proper venting hole in the top crust is essential. The filling expands as it warms and if the vent is too small the top crust will lift right off the bottom. Cut a ¼-inch vent in the middle of half the rounds (these will be the top crusts) using a tiny fondant cutter, the tip of a chopstick, the smaller end of a pastry tip, or a straw, making sure the hole remains open when the popper is topped. The opening is likely to stretch as you cover the filling, so keep the initial vent small. Place the forms on a baking sheet and chill for at least 20 minutes before filling. In fact, just get in the habit of chilling at every step along the way. Working with cold dough is always easier.

Forming one popper at a time, working with cold filling, brush the edges of one round with egg wash. Place a scant, packed 1 tablespoon of filling on one of the rounds; I like to use a scoop for portioning—it compacts the filling, which helps ensure enough filling gets into the popper.

Lift a vented round and place over the filling, covering the bottom round. Work your way around the pie, pinching the edges closed while also releasing any air bubbles around the filling. I like to hold the bottom round in my palm and form the pie in my hand. Others like to work on the board. You will find what is most comfortable for you.

Transfer the popper to the baking sheet and firmly crimp the edges with a fork. This crimp is essential. Taking care not to overfill, and to thoroughly crimp the edges will help ensure they stay together. Repeat until there are 12 poppers on the baking sheet. Brush the tops with egg wash. Refrigerate or freeze while repeating the process with the other block of pie dough, making an additional 12 poppers.

SAUCING

Poppers love a good dipping sauce: A sweet chile sauce elevates the Crab Rangoon Pie Poppers (page 79) and I serve turkey poppers with hot, sweet mustard. With sweet poppers? Warm the Caramelized Banana and Nutella Pie Poppers (page 85) and tuck them into a bowl of vanilla ice cream for a new spin on the banana split.

STORING, FREEZING, AND REHEATING

As with every other type of pie, chilling the formed poppers will help them hold their shape and bake up beautifully. And because poppers are a little bit of work, I will double or triple the recipe. Keep ziptop bags of frozen poppers available to slip into the oven at the drop of a hat.

To freeze unbaked poppers, first spread them out on a baking sheet and freeze them solid (about 40 minutes), and then slide them into a ziptop bag and keep in the freezer for up to 3 months. Bake frozen pie poppers for about the same amount of time in the recipe. Visual cues (bubbling filling, browning crust) are always the best indication of doneness.

CARRY ON

If the **filling is oozing from the sides** of the popper, check the venting hole—it likely needs to be slightly larger.

If the **filling is volcano-ing out of the top** of the popper, check the venting hole—it likely needs to be slightly smaller.

Does the top pop off the bottom in the oven? Do not overfill because the crimp will not hold the poppers together. Use only a scant 1 tablespoon filling, but, at the same time, pack the filling into the tablespoon measure. A scoop is very helpful.

Is the dough tough and chewy instead of flaky and tender? **Make sure the filling is cold** and that the dough doesn't warm as you are stretching it over the filling. And be sure to chill the poppers hard before baking.

Taste the filling before making the poppers. **The flavors should be bold.** Even if it's a little too salty, too spicy, too sweet—that's okay because there's a lot of crust and the filling has to stand up and be noticed.

Bake until really deeply golden brown or risk limp poppers.

THANKSGIVING-IN-A-BITE PIE POPPERS

Makes 24

2 slices (2 ounces, 56 g) thick-cut smoked bacon, diced

2 tablespoons thinly sliced scallion (white and green parts)

½ pound (225 g) ground turkey, light and dark meat

½ teaspoon fresh thyme leaves

½ teaspoon dried sage

½ teaspoon kosher salt

¼ teaspoon freshly ground black pepper

½ cup (70 g) frozen peas

½ cup (57 g) toasted pepitas (shelled pumpkin seeds)

½ cup (57 g) cranberry sauce

¼ cup (56 g) mayonnaise or full-fat Greek yogurt

2 recipes All-Butter Pie Dough, page 251, formed into 3- by 4-inch rectangular blocks

Egg wash (1 egg beaten with 1 tablespoon cool water and ¼ teaspoon kosher salt)

Sweet 'n' Hot Mustard Sauce (recipe follows), for serving (optional)

One of the great American holiday institutions is the after-Thanksgiving sandwich. Inspired by the idea of re-creating those delicious flavors into a pie bite, I played with different parts of the classic menu as filling ingredients. Sweet potatoes were mushy, and mushrooms were rubbery. But I found that cranberries added an acidic bite that was needed and pepitas gave needed crunch. During (and after) the holiday season, these poppers are a flavor-filled pass-around.

In a large skillet over medium heat, fry the bacon until crisp. Transfer the bacon with a slotted spoon to a medium bowl. Add the scallions to the fat in the pan and cook until the edges have turned deep brown, 4 to 5 minutes. Add the turkey, breaking it up with two wooden spoons until crumbly and no longer pink. Add the thyme, sage, salt, and pepper and cook, stirring, until well combined and smelling like Thanksgiving, 3 or 4 minutes. Scrape the turkey mixture into the bowl with the bacon and fold gently until thoroughly mixed. Cool completely. Stir in the peas, pepitas, cranberry sauce, and mayonnaise.

Place a Baking Steel, baking stone, or inverted baking sheet on the center rack and heat the oven to 375°F. Line two baking sheets with parchment.

Remove one block of dough from the refrigerator. Roll out the dough to an approximate 9- by 13-inch rectangle, cut out 24 (2-inch) rounds, and vent half of them. Brush the edge of one round with egg wash. Add a scant, packed 1 tablespoon filling and form a popper with a second (vented) round. Transfer to a baking sheet and firmly fork-crimp the edges. (See Forming, Crimping, and Venting Pie Poppers, page 74, for complete instructions.)

Continue to make 12 poppers. Brush the surface of each with egg wash. Refrigerate or freeze while repeating the process with the other block of pie dough to make a total of 24 poppers.

Bake the poppers for 20 to 25 minutes, until deeply golden brown. I prefer to bake them one baking sheet at a time to take advantage of the Baking Steel in my oven, but if you want to bake them at the same time, switch them top to bottom and front to back halfway through the bake. Serve warm or at room temperature, with the mustard sauce, if you like.

SWEET 'N' HOT MUSTARD SAUCE

Makes 1 cup

⅓ cup (65 g) granulated sugar

2 teaspoons all-purpose flour

2 teaspoons Coleman's mustard powder

½ cup (120 ml) milk

1 large egg yolk

¼ cup (60 ml) white wine vinegar

If you've ever had a ham biscuit, this hot and sweet mustard sauce is often served alongside. It's perfect with ham, but also with turkey, thick and tangy and full of zesty flavor.

In a small bowl, blend the sugar, flour, and mustard powder. In a small saucepan, whisk the milk and egg yolk until combined. Place over medium heat and slowly add the flour mixture and the vinegar. Without stopping whisking, bring the mixture to a boil. Reduce the heat to low and cook for 2 minutes, until thickened. The sauce may be kept, covered, in the refrigerator for a week.

CRAB RANGOON PIE POPPERS

Makes 24

¼ cup (25 g) finely chopped scallions

Juice of 1 lemon

2 teaspoons Worcestershire sauce

1 teaspoon tamari or low-sodium soy sauce

½ teaspoon grated garlic

½ teaspoon Sriracha hot sauce (optional)

¼ teaspoon freshly ground black pepper

8 tablespoons (4 ounces, 113 g) cream cheese, cubed

---

8 ounces (225 g) fresh crab meat, carefully picked over to remove any shell and cartilage

---

2 recipes Cream Cheese Pie Dough, page 252, formed into 3- by 4-inch rectangular blocks

Egg wash (1 egg beaten with 1 tablespoon cool water and ¼ teaspoon kosher salt)

Spicy Chile Caramel Sauce (recipe follows), for serving

America's version of Chinese food was very uncomplicated in my Midwestern childhood. The choices were limited: chop suey, sweet and sour pork, wonton soup, sticky riblets, and crab rangoon. Even at five years old, I loved the rich filling surrounded by crisp wonton wrappers, dipped in fiery sauce. I have never lost my love for crab rangoon, so I made a pie-adjacent version, including that very special sauce.

Stir together the scallions, lemon juice, Worcestershire sauce, tamari, garlic, Sriracha (if using), and black pepper in a wide bowl. Let sit for 10 minutes to relax the sharpness of the scallion and garlic. Whisk in the cream cheese, one piece at a time, until the mixture is smooth-ish. Fold in the crab. Cover and refrigerate until ready to fill the poppers.

Place a Baking Steel, baking stone, or inverted baking sheet on the center rack and heat the oven to 375°F. Line two baking sheets with parchment.

Remove one block of dough from the refrigerator. Roll out the dough to an approximate 9- by 13-inch rectangle, cut out 24 (2-inch) rounds, and vent half of them. Brush the edge of one round with egg wash. Add a scant, packed 1 tablespoon filling to one round and form a popper with a second (vented) round. Transfer to a baking sheet and firmly fork-crimp the edges. (See Forming, Crimping, and Venting Pie Poppers, page 74, for complete instructions.)

Continue to make 12 poppers. Brush the surface of each with egg wash. Refrigerate or freeze while repeating the process with the other block of pie dough to make a total of 24 poppers.

Bake the poppers for 20 to 25 minutes, until deeply golden brown. I prefer to bake the pies one baking sheet at a time to take advantage of the Baking steel in my oven, but if you want to bake them at the same time, switch them top to bottom and front to back halfway through the bake.

Serve warm. They are traditionally served (and are most delicious) with the Spicy Chile Caramel Sauce.

SPICY CHILE CARAMEL SAUCE

Makes 1 cup

¾ cup (150 g) granulated sugar

¼ cup (60 ml) rice vinegar

½ cup (120 ml) water

2 small Thai chiles, seeded and finely chopped, or 1½ teaspoons crushed red pepper flakes

2 garlic cloves, finely chopped

2 tablespoons cornstarch

This sauce packs a punch and dazzles with the rich, smooth crab rangoon poppers. Do not expect a dark, rich caramel. This is an opaque, milky sauce, lovely and incendiary. I like to serve it slightly warmed.

Combine the sugar, vinegar, and ¼ cup of the water in a small saucepan over medium-high heat, stir well, and bring to a boil. Cook until the mixture begins to take on some caramel tones, just slightly golden, 4 to 6 minutes. Remove from the heat and stir in the chiles and garlic. Cover and steep for 20 minutes.

In a small bowl, stir together the cornstarch and remaining ¼ cup water until smooth. Add to the caramel sauce and return to medium-high heat. Stir without stopping until the mixture comes to a strong boil. Boil hard, continuing to stir, for exactly 1 minute. The mixture will thicken and turn opaque. Remove the pan from the heat and let the sauce thicken further as it cools slightly. Serve warm-ish.

The sauce can be made ahead and stored in a covered dish or jar in the refrigerator for up to 1 week. Reheat gently.

KOREAN BO SSAM AND KIMCHI PIE POPPERS

Makes 24

½ pound (225 g) ground pork

2 tablespoons sliced scallion (white and green parts)

1 tablespoon grated fresh ginger

1 teaspoon grated garlic

1 tablespoon soy sauce

1½ tablespoons rice wine vinegar

1 tablespoon gochujang paste

1 tablespoon toasted sesame oil

1 tablespoon granulated sugar

½ cup (110 g) kimchi, drained well and roughly chopped

2 recipes All-Butter Pie Dough, page 251, formed into 3- by 4-inch rectangular blocks

Egg wash (1 egg beaten with 1 tablespoon cool water and ¼ teaspoon kosher salt)

Scallion Sauce (recipe follows), for serving (optional)

Bo ssam is a wonderful party food—a huge hunk of slow-roasted pork shoulder surrounded by a raft of Korean condiments and fresh herbs. It's mouth-watering joy on a plate. To re-create the bo ssam experience as a pie, ground pork is mixed with aromatics and the stinging heat of gochujang, a fiery chile paste, along with plenty of fermented funk and crunch from kimchi.

In a large skillet over medium heat, cook the pork, breaking it up, until crumbly and no longer pink. Add the scallion, ginger, and garlic and cook for a minute or two, until the scents of ginger and garlic bloom. Stir in the soy sauce, vinegar, gochujang, sesame oil, and sugar. Simmer until most of the liquid has evaporated, about 5 minutes. Scrape the mixture into a bowl and cool completely. Stir in the kimchi.

Place a Baking Steel, baking stone, or inverted baking sheet on the center rack and heat the oven to 375°F. Line two baking sheets with parchment.

Remove one block of dough from the refrigerator. Roll out the dough to an approximate 9- by 13-inch rectangle, cut out 24 (2-inch) rounds, and vent half of them. Brush the edge of one round with egg wash. Add a scant, packed 1 tablespoon filling to one round and form a popper with a second (vented) round. Transfer to a baking sheet and firmly fork-crimp the edges. (See Forming, Crimping, and Venting Pie Poppers, page 74, for complete instructions.)

Continue to make 12 poppers. Brush the surface of each with egg wash. Refrigerate or freeze while repeating the process with the other block of pie dough to make a total of 24 poppers.

(Continued)

Bake the poppers for 20 to 25 minutes, until deeply golden brown. I prefer to bake the pies one baking sheet at a time, to take advantage of the Baking Steel in my oven, but if you want to bake them at the same time, switch them top to bottom and front to back halfway through the bake.

Serve warm with the Scallion Sauce.

SCALLION SAUCE

Makes about 1 cup

½ cup (120 ml) grapeseed or canola oil

½ cup (50 g) thinly sliced scallions (about 4), white and green parts

1 tablespoon grated fresh ginger

1 teaspoon tamari or low-sodium soy sauce

1 teaspoon rice wine vinegar

1 teaspoon gochujang paste

¼ teaspoon kosher salt

A fiery dipping sauce for bo ssam poppers.

Combine the oil, scallions, ginger, tamari, vinegar, gochujang, and salt in a jar with a lid. Shake until combined. Chill until ready to use, at least 1 hour.

CARAMELIZED BANANA AND NUTELLA PIE POPPERS

Makes 24

3 tablespoons (42 g) unsalted butter

4 slightly overripe medium bananas, sliced in half vertically

3 tablespoons packed brown sugar

⅛ teaspoon kosher salt

2 tablespoons dark rum (Myers's and Gosling's are my favorites)

¼ cup (75 g) Nutella or another chocolate and hazelnut spread

2 recipes Chocolate Pie Dough, page 256, formed into 3- by 4-inch rectangular blocks

Egg wash (1 egg beaten with 1 tablespoon cool water and ¼ teaspoon kosher salt)

Sparkling sugar

Bananas laced with rum only get better with Nutella. This reminds me of s'mores and bananas Foster, all wrapped up in one. They're sweet and intense and a great summertime treat as a topper for ice cream. Let the bananas develop some color and sticky goodness for the toasty flavor I consider essential. A nonstick pan is a must. No joke.

In a nonstick skillet in which the halved bananas will fit without crowding, melt the butter over medium-high heat until it begins to foam. Add the bananas, cut sides down, and cook until deeply browned, then turn and do the same on the other side. The whole process should take about 5 minutes, depending on how ripe the bananas are. Add the brown sugar and salt and swirl the pan and stir until the sugar is dissolved and bubbling. It's sticky and messy, but carry on. Add the rum. Stir well and scrape the bananas and all the melted butter and sugar into a bowl. Use a fork to mash the banana into smaller pieces. Cool the mixture, then stir in the Nutella, leaving the filling streaked and not overly mixed.

Place a Baking Steel, baking stone, or inverted baking sheet on the center rack and heat the oven to 375°F. Line two baking sheets with parchment.

Remove one block of dough from the refrigerator. Roll out the dough to an approximate 9- by 13-inch rectangle, cut out 24 (2-inch) squares, and vent half of them. Brush the edges of one square with the egg wash. Add a scant, packed 1 tablespoon filling to one round and top the popper with a second (vented) round. Transfer to a baking sheet and firmly

(Continued)

fork-crimp the edges. (See Forming, Crimping, and Venting Pie Poppers, page 74, for complete instructions.)

Continue to make 12 poppers. Brush the surface of each with egg wash and dust with sparkling sugar. Refrigerate or freeze while repeating the process with the other block of pie dough to make a total of 24 poppers.

Bake the poppers for 20 to 25 minutes, until deeply golden brown. I prefer to bake the pies one baking sheet at a time, but if you want to bake them at the same time, switch them top to bottom and front to back halfway through the bake.

Serve warm or at room temperature.

PBJ PIE POPPERS

Makes 24

¼ cup (72 g) peanut butter

4 tablespoons (2 ounces, 56 g) cream cheese

½ cup (56 g) powdered sugar

1 tablespoon heavy cream

¼ cup (30 g) salted peanuts, chopped

⅓ cup (84 g) grape jelly (or any other jelly or jam)

2 recipes All-Butter Pie Dough, page 251, formed into 3- by 4-inch rectangular blocks

Egg wash (1 egg beaten with 1 tablespoon cool water and ¼ teaspoon kosher salt)

Sparkling sugar

These poppers taste like the best peanut butter and jelly sandwich on toast—perfect for kids' parties, after-school treats, and picnic fare. Opt for commercial peanut butter (Jif or Skippy) for the best results. I'm a sucker for grape jelly, but try strawberry or peach, or cherry jam. Make no other substitutions. This recipe was surprisingly challenging to sort out and does not work with alternative nut butters.

In the bowl of a stand mixer, or with a stiff spoon, beat the peanut butter and cream cheese with the powdered sugar and cream until smooth and fluffy. Stir in the peanuts and then swirl in the jelly. Do not overblend.

Place a Baking Steel, baking stone, or inverted baking sheet on the center rack and heat the oven to 375°F. Line two baking sheets with parchment.

Remove one block of dough from the refrigerator. Roll out the dough to an approximate 9- by 13-inch rectangle, cut out 24 (2-inch) rounds, and vent half of them. Add a packed scant 1 tablespoon filling to one round and form a popper with a second (vented) round. Transfer to a baking sheet and firmly fork-crimp the edges. (See Forming, Crimping, and Venting Pie Poppers, page 74, for complete instructions.)

Continue to make 12 poppers. Brush the surface of each with egg wash and dust enthusiastically with sparkling sugar. Refrigerate or freeze while repeating the process with the other block of pie dough to make a total of 24 poppers.

Bake the poppers for 20 to 25 minutes, until deeply golden brown. I prefer to bake the pies one baking sheet at a time to take advantage of the Baking Steel in my oven, but if you want to bake them at the same time, switch them top to bottom and front to back halfway through the bake.

Let the filling cool before serving.

BRANDIED PEACH PIE POPPERS

Makes 24

1½ cups (112g) peeled and pitted peaches, chopped into ½-inch cubes (about 3 medium)

1 tablespoon lemon juice

¾ cup (180 ml) water

¾ cup (150 g) granulated sugar

⅓ cup (80 ml) brandy

½ teaspoon ground cinnamon

2 tablespoons cornstarch whisked with 2 tablespoons cool water

2 recipes Cream Cheese Pie Dough, page 252, formed into 3- by 4-inch rectangular blocks

Egg wash (1 egg beaten with 1 tablespoon cool water and ¼ teaspoon kosher salt)

2 tablespoons cold milk

½ teaspoon vanilla extract

2 cups (225 g) powdered sugar

Peaches—ripe, juicy, and scented—are exquisite summer treats. A peach pie is a seasonal highlight. Poppers need extra flavor, though, so I took a hint from those boozy flavor bombs, brandied peaches, something my great-grandmother kept in jars on the basement steps. Here, the peaches are cooked until jammy and sweet, then take a brandy bath for a heady finish to a devilishly delicious filling. If you'd rather not make these boozy, just skip the brandy altogether and add 1 teaspoon vanilla extract instead, for a sweet peach popper that tastes like a glorious summer pie in a single bite.

Toss the chopped peaches with the lemon juice to keep the fruit from browning. In a 3-quart saucepan, heat the water and granulated sugar over high heat until boiling. Continue to boil to reduce the syrup by half, about 8 minutes. Cool slightly. Pour the syrup over the peaches, stir in the brandy, and cover. Let the peaches hang out and get boozy overnight in the refrigerator.

With a slotted spoon, remove the peaches and set aside in a small bowl. Return the syrup to the saucepan, bring to a boil over high heat, and cook until reduced to about ½ cup (120 ml), 10 to 12 minutes. Add the peaches, return to a boil, then stir in the cinnamon and cornstarch mixture. Bring back to a boil and boil for exactly 1 minute. Scrape the peach filling into a bowl (to stop the cooking) and cool thoroughly before forming the poppers. Cover and refrigerate the filling for up to a week or freeze for up to 6 months.

Place a Baking Steel, baking stone, or inverted baking sheet on the center rack and heat the oven to 375°F. Line two baking sheets with parchment.

(Continued)

Remove one block of dough from the refrigerator. Roll out the dough to an approximate 9- by 13-inch rectangle, cut out 24 (2-inch) rounds, and vent half of them. Brush the edge of one round with egg wash. Add a packed scant 1 tablespoon filling to one round and form a popper with a second (vented) round. Transfer to a baking sheet and firmly fork-crimp the edges. (See Forming, Crimping, and Venting Pie Poppers, page 74, for complete instructions.)

Continue to make 12 poppers. Brush the surface of each with egg wash. Refrigerate or freeze while repeating the process with the other block of pie dough to make a total of 24 poppers.

Bake the poppers for 20 to 25 minutes, until deeply golden brown. I prefer to bake the poppers one baking sheet at a time, to take advantage of the Baking Steel in my oven, but if you want to bake them at the same time, switch them top to bottom and front to back halfway through the bake.

Whisk the milk and vanilla extract together and then whisk in the powdered sugar until smooth and very thick. If it isn't coming together, dribble in the tiniest additional amount of milk. If it's too thin, add a little more powdered sugar. Transfer to a pastry bag or ziptop bag, snip off a corner, and squiggle the frosting across the surface of each pie. (Or use an offset spatula to spread the frosting evenly across the surface of each popper, inside the crimped edges.) Let the frosting set up, about 30 minutes, before serving.

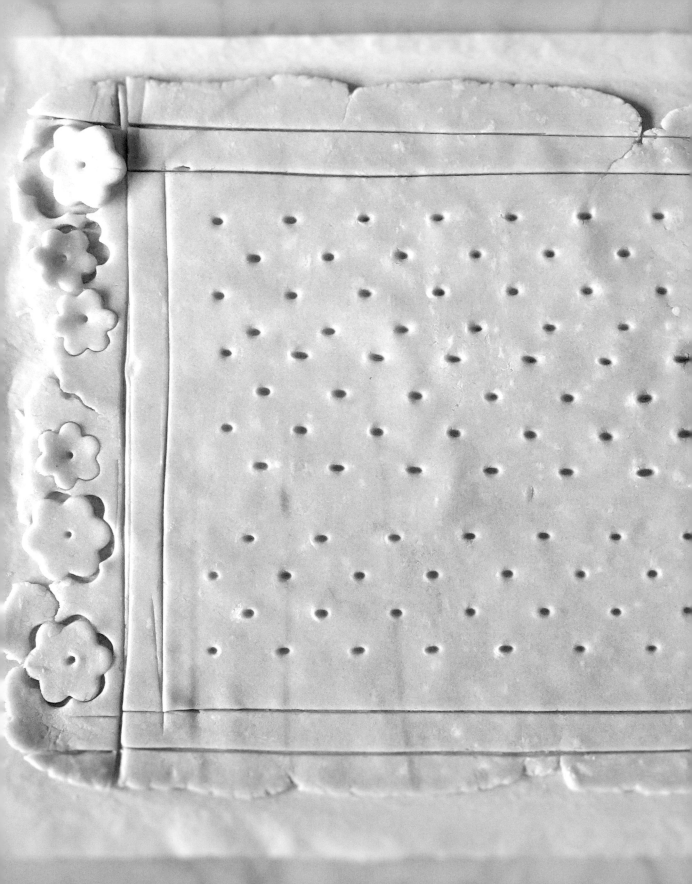

CHAPTER 4

FRAMED TARTS
DECORATED PIES

There are many ways to make a tart and this chapter covers my mother's way. Free form, and an expression of the cook's creativity, these are tarts that need no pan. The dough is rolled flat and decorated as though it were a picture frame, with shallow, ornamental edges made of layers of dough, then filled with carefully placed ingredients. Rich, beautiful, and dramatic, these are pie-adjacent options for lunch, a main course, or dazzling dessert.

Tarts are most often associated with precious French pastries. With fluted sides made of sweet pâte brisée, they are made in pans with removable bottoms (the ones that go missing). I make those tarts, but they're for another time. In this context, I am making my mother's version of a tart. Roll out a generous piece of dough and trim a precise size, whether round or square, rectangular or octagonal, for a flat, crispy, flaky pastry base. Then make raised edges from the trimmings, decorating the corners with aplomb.

In this chapter, the bases are baked unfilled, a practice called blind baking. And fillings are constructed like a game of Jenga. I realize tarts in this context may seem a little fussy. There are recipes within recipes. There are spreads and schmears. I'll admit there is some specificity to the instructions. For the Glazed Fruit Tart (page 127), I delicately place the fruit, one little berry at a time, across a pastry cream.

The tart, unlike the galette's rough and tumble character, is refined, particular, and pretty as a picture. The Sour Cherry Stuffed-Crust Tart (page 123) may take a little more work, but delivers a self-sustaining, entirely contained cherry pie, without a pan. Just watch your guests' eyes open wide at the fruit-filled crust.

Have fun with these tarts—they're an expression of joy and a delight to deliver tableside. Behold the tart, a flat pastry upon which layers of deliciousness form a worthy still life.

The crusts for tarts may be found on pages 251 to 259.

FORMING THE EDGE

Framed, a tart may take on any shape. The base is rolled and trimmed to size. The trimmings are then the basis for cut-out decorative edges that provide some whimsy as well as a frame for the filling—make note that these edges will not hold back a flood of filling.

I use a pizza wheel, fluted pastry wheel, cookie cutters, and fondant cutters to make attractive edging on these tart-like forms. Alphabet cutters are amusing. Leaf shapes are beautiful. Tiny hearts, stars, and flowers are endearing.

Roll the trimmings out just a little, flattening the dough, so there's a bit more area to play with, then cut out small shapes. Paint the edge of the dough with egg wash and place your cutouts. They do not need to touch each other. Remember—they are not there for holding back enthusiastic fillings—they are merely pretty. Pay particular attention to the corners (which will be the most visible) and have fun, layering flower on flower, stars over hearts.

LAYERING

To expect a blind-baked crust to support a number of weighty ingredients is asking a lot. Can it support slices of pork tenderloin (Banh Mi–Style Caramel Pork Tart, page 111)? Will it hold an egg in a prosciutto cup (Crisped Kale and Baked Egg Tart, page 109)? The secret is to keep the crust from becoming soggy or soupy. There are two ways to work this out. First, blind bake the shell on a hot surface—a Baking Steel, baking stone, or inverted baking sheet heated with the oven.

Next, protect that crispy layer from any sauciness with a schmear of mayonnaise, cream cheese, or mascarpone. Think of these framed tarts as a bit of architecture, with the schmear being the mortar providing moisture control. Above it, the filling must be bold and textural, with strong flavors. Consider pastry cream's unctuousness against the burst of sugared fresh fruit. The elements in the filling should be bite-sized and tender, so eating it is not a challenge.

Make the shape match the servings, with long rectangular tarts portioning out to 4 square slabs (Crisped Kale and Baked Egg Tart, page 109), or a round of cheesy tomatoes (Roasted Tomato Quattro-Formaggio Tart, page 105) divided into wedges like its cousin, the pizza. I've even fashioned the Millionaire's Tart (page 130) into a heart for a sweetheart of a pie that portions into 8 little wedges.

FLIGHT PLANS. MAKE A STENCIL.

At times, I have fun with the form. Consider the Millionaire's Tart (page 130) and its heart-shaped base. I cut out a bagel shape for Sunday's Lox and Schmear Tart (page 103). Consider a fish or a sailboat and use parchment paper to sketch out the shape. If you have extensive decorations in mind, consider starting with an extra disk of dough.

CARRY ON

Use a paring knife or pizza wheel to lightly **score the base before baking,** making indentations where the tart will be portioned. Once baked, the tart will be easier to serve.

The edges of any blind-baked pie will be susceptible to overbaking, growing more than golden brown, even blackening. (This is especially true with Caramelized Onion and Cheese Pie Dough, page 259, and Brown-Butter Pie Dough, page 254.) Avoid this by using strips of foil to **tent the edges** during the last 5 to 10 minutes of baking.

Do not overfill or the tart will be messy to eat. These tarts are best when sparely layered with glorious ingredients.

Serve immediately. These tarts do not benefit from sitting around and cannot be made ahead. The blind-baked base may be made in advance.

It's worth it to give in to your inner quiet space, **get Zen,** and spend time decorating a tart. Each one has the potential to be a showstopper.

BLIND BAKING

Blind baking refers to pre-baking a pie or tart crust. It's the best solution if the filling needs only a brief moment under the broiler, as in the Roasted Tomato Quattro-Formaggio Tart (page 105) or will not be cooked further after filling, as in the Banh Mi–Style Caramel Pork Tart (page 111).

A blind-baked tart crust may be made a day in advance. Cover with plastic wrap and leave it on the counter, not in the refrigerator. This make-ahead magic will come in very handy.

Prepare the pie dough as directed in the recipe and roll it out. Then, drape the dough over the rolling pin and unroll it on to a parchment-lined baking sheet. Form the edges with the trimmed dough, as described above. Chill the framed base for 20 to 30 minutes. Place a Baking Steel, baking stone, or inverted baking sheet on the center rack and heat the oven to 375°F.

Pierce the base, not the edges, of the pastry all over—a practice called docking—using a fork or docking tool. Docking will keep the pastry from bubbling and blistering as it bakes.

Brush the edges with egg wash. Line the unbaked crust with foil or parchment paper (lightly coated with cooking spray on the side that will be in contact with the dough), allowing for plenty of overhang for easy lifting. Fill generously with pie weights, uncooked beans, raw rice, pennies, or granulated sugar, keeping the decorated edges free of the weights. (Credit Stella Parks for the sugar idea. When you're done, you'll have toasted sugar, which can be used in any baking recipe for a slight caramel flavor.)

For a par-baked tart crust (if the tart will be baked again): Blind bake the crust for 10 minutes, until lightly golden on the edges. Carefully remove the paper holding the weights and pop the pan back in the oven to dry out the pastry, about 10 more minutes.

For a fully baked tart crust (if the tart will not be baked again after filling): Blind bake the crust for 20 minutes, until golden brown and crisp on the edges. Carefully remove the paper holding the weights and pop the pan back in the oven to dry out the pastry, about 10 more minutes.

Cool the crust in the pan on a rack. It may be baked a few hours, or even a day, in advance and kept covered on the counter, awaiting filling. Do not refrigerate.

Hold on to those pie weights, whether dried beans or pennies. I keep mine in a jar and use them over and over. If you use sugar, you'll have toasted sugar, which may be used in any recipe for a light caramel flavor.

SUNDAY'S LOX AND SCHMEAR TART

Serves 8

1 recipe Everything Spice Pie Dough (page 257), formed into a disk

Egg wash (1 egg beaten with 1 tablespoon cool water and ¼ teaspoon kosher salt)

¼ cup (35 g) finely chopped red onion

¼ cup (60 ml) cool water

4 tablespoons (2 ounces, 56 g) cream cheese

¼ cup (25 g) sliced scallions, white and green parts (about 2)

3 tablespoons snipped fresh chives, plus extra for garnish

1 tablespoon finely chopped fresh flat-leaf parsley

1 tablespoon freshly squeezed lemon juice

¼ teaspoon kosher salt

1 baseball-sized (225 g, 8 ounces), perfectly ripe tomato, thinly sliced or chopped and drained

4 ounces (113 g) Nova lox or smoked salmon, slivered

1 tablespoon capers, rinsed

1 lemon, sliced into 8 wedges

Have some fun at your next brunch: Forego the bagels and make a bagel tart instead. I like to shape this like an actual bagel, round with a hole in the center, with small bagel-shaped cutouts skirting the edge. It's fun and silly and delicious all at once, and it demands a Bloody Mary and half-sour pickle as an accompaniment.

Line a baking sheet with parchment. Lightly dust the counter with flour and roll the dough to a 12-inch round. With a paring knife or pizza wheel, trim to a 10-inch round. Lift the dough using a bench scraper or offset spatula and briskly transfer to the baking sheet; roll it over the pin or fold it gently, do what's needed—be brave and adjust the shape as needed after moving.

Cut out a round in the center of the dough about 3 inches in diameter, using a glass or a cookie cutter, so the tart shell looks like an oversized bagel. With a small round cutter (I used the large end of a pastry tip), cut out small rounds from the dough trimmings and the center cutout, then make tiny holes in the centers (with the small end of the pastry tip or a bamboo skewer) to make small bagel shapes.

Pierce the dough all over with a fork or a docking tool. Brush the edge of the bagel circle with egg wash and place the tiny bagels atop the edge, decoratively. Brush the edges with egg wash. Chill the dough for 20 to 30 minutes.

Place a Baking Steel, baking stone, or inverted baking sheet on the center rack and heat the oven to 400°F.

Cut a piece of foil or parchment paper slightly larger than the size of the dough and spray one side with cooking spray. Lay it on top of the unbaked crust with the sprayed side facing down. Make sure there is enough paper overhanging the edges of the dough for easy lifting later. Fill generously with pie weights, uncooked beans, raw rice, pennies, or granulated sugar, keeping the decorated edges free of the weights.

Bake with the weights for 20 minutes, until golden brown and crisp on the edges.

Carefully remove the paper holding the weights and pop the pastry back in the oven to dry out the pie crust, about 10 more minutes.

Cool the crust in the pan on a rack. It may be baked a few hours, or even a day, in advance and kept covered on the counter, awaiting filling. Do not refrigerate.

Combine the onion and water in a small bowl and let soak for at least 5 minutes. This will remove any sharpness. In a medium bowl, use a sturdy spoon to beat the cream cheese until lightened, then add the scallions, chives, parsley, lemon juice, and salt and mix well.

To assemble the tart, drain the water from the onions and dry them well on a paper towel. Spread the cream cheese mixture across the tart shell with an offset spatula. Decoratively place the thin slices of tomato all around and mound the slivered salmon over the tomato. Top with the red onion and capers, garnish with chives, and serve with lemon wedges.

ROASTED TOMATO QUATTRO-FORMAGGIO TART

Serves 6

1 recipe Caramelized Onion and Cheese Pie Dough (page 259), formed into a disk

Egg wash (1 egg beaten with 1 tablespoon cool water and ¼ teaspoon kosher salt)

1 pint plump cherry tomatoes, anywhere from 15 to 30, depending on size

½ cup (120 ml) olive oil

2 stalks fresh rosemary

3 garlic cloves, smashed and peeled

½ teaspoon crushed red pepper flakes

¾ teaspoon kosher salt

2 cups (120 g) fresh basil leaves

½ cup (56 g) shredded fresh mozzarella

1 ounce (28 g) crumbled Gorgonzola

3 ounces (85 g) sliced provolone (about 6 slices)

2 tablespoons grated Parmigiano Reggiano

When summer reaches its zenith and boxes of cherry tomatoes form a sea of red and yellow and deep maroon on the farmers' market tables, this tart is where my mind goes. Roasting cherry tomatoes is a smart summer technique, tripling the tomatoes' sweetness while the color stays true. My advice? Double the tomatoes you roast because you will snack. This pretty tart is ideal for a summer supper with steamed corn on the cob and grilled peaches. Be aware—the onion and cheese pie dough browns quickly. Once the pie is under the broiler, you may want to cover the edges in foil—and watch it like a hawk—to avoid burning.

Line a baking sheet with parchment. Lightly dust the counter with flour and roll the dough into a scant 12-inch round. Trim and tidy the dough to a 10-inch round using a paring knife, pizza wheel, or decorative pastry wheel. Lift the dough using a bench scraper or offset spatula, roll it around the pin or fold it lightly, and briskly transfer it to the baking sheet; be brave and adjust the shape as needed after moving. Turn about ½ inch of the outside edge toward the center of the dough round to make a slightly raised border. This is the simplest decorative edge; if you want something fancier, refer to the other tarts in this chapter.

Pierce the center of the dough all over with a fork or docking tool. Brush the edges with egg wash. Chill the dough for 30 minutes.

Place a Baking Steel, baking stone, or inverted baking sheet on the center rack and heat the oven to 375°F.

Cut a piece of foil or parchment paper slightly larger than

(Continued)

the size of the dough and spray one side with cooking spray. Place it on top of the unbaked crust with the sprayed side facing down. Make sure there is enough paper overhanging the edges of the dough for easy lifting later. Fill generously with pie weights, uncooked beans, raw rice, pennies, or granulated sugar, keeping the decorated edges free of the weights.

Bake with the weights for 10 minutes, until golden brown and crisp on the edges.

Carefully remove the paper holding the weights and pop the pastry back in the oven to dry out the crust, about 10 more minutes.

Cool the crust in the pan on a rack. It may be baked a few hours, or even a day, in advance and kept covered on the counter, awaiting filling. Do not refrigerate.

Increase the oven temperature to 425°F. Toss the cherry tomatoes with ¼ cup (60 ml) of the oil and spread them out on an unlined baking sheet. Nestle the rosemary and garlic cloves around the tomatoes and sprinkle with the red pepper flakes and ½ teaspoon salt. Roast for 20 minutes, until the tomatoes have started to collapse. Remove and discard the rosemary and garlic and cool the tomatoes completely. The tomatoes may be roasted up to 3 days in advance and kept covered in the refrigerator.

Place a rack in the uppermost part of the oven and heat to broil. In a food processor or mortar and pestle, chop the basil and remaining ¼ cup (60 ml) olive oil and ¼ teaspoon salt until a smooth paste is formed. Avoiding the edges, use an offset spatula to spread half of the basil paste across the tart (reserve the other half for sandwiches or spooning over grilled or roasted vegetables). Scatter the mozzarella and Gorgonzola across the base. Layer the provolone slices on top of the cheeses.

If necessary, use a slotted spoon to lift the tomatoes from the oil and scatter them across the tart. (Reserve the oil to brush on vegetables, poultry, meat, or fish before roasting.) Sprinkle the tomatoes with Parmigiano Reggiano. Slide the pie under the broiler and broil until the cheeses are starting to brown and everything is bubbly, 4 to 6 minutes.

Cool the tart briefly before serving to let the cheese firm up a bit; it will be easier to slice.

CRISPED KALE AND BAKED EGG TART

Serves 4

---

1 recipe All-Butter Pie Dough, page 251, formed into a 3- by 4-inch rectangular block

Egg wash (1 egg beaten with 1 tablespoon cool water and ¼ teaspoon kosher salt)

6 ounces (170 g) lacinato or another flat-leaved kale

2 tablespoons (28 g) unsalted butter

1 teaspoon minced shallot

⅓ cup (80 ml) crème fraîche

¼ teaspoon smoked paprika

1 tablespoon olive oil

8 pieces very thinly sliced prosciutto (about 5 ounces, 140 g)

4 large eggs

4 tablespoons heavy cream

¼ cup (35 g) toasted hazelnuts, chopped

¼ cup (28 g) grated Parmigiano Reggiano

This picture-perfect tart is welcome for a light supper or brunch. To keep the eggs in place, form the prosciutto nests, pinching the base together, so there are no gaping seams through which the egg and cream can escape, and move the tart into the oven without delay. With the vegetal bite of a kale salad below, a lacy surface that mimics kale chips, and creamy baked eggs, you need nothing but a glass of bright white wine to complete the meal. Very important: The eggs will not cook properly in a convection oven. Bake this conventionally, in the center of the oven, without the fan.

Line a baking sheet with parchment. Lightly dust the counter with flour and roll the dough into an approximate 6- by 10-inch rectangle. Trim and tidy to 4 by 9 inches with a paring knife, pizza wheel, or decorative pastry wheel. Lift the dough using a bench scraper or offset spatula, fold gently, and briskly transfer to the baking sheet; be brave and adjust the shape as needed after moving.

Roll out the dough trimmings and slice into long pieces to create long and solid edges around the base of the dough rectangle. You'll want this to help support the egg cups. Use the egg wash as glue and stack the pieces along the edges. Pierce the center of the dough all over with a fork or a docking tool. Brush the edges with egg wash. Chill for 20 to 30 minutes.

Place a Baking Steel, baking stone, or inverted baking sheet on the center rack and heat the oven to 375°F.

Cut a piece of foil or parchment paper slightly larger than the size of the dough and spray one side with cooking spray. Lay it on top of the unbaked crust with the sprayed side facing down. Make sure there is enough paper overhanging the edges of the dough for easy lifting later. Fill generously with pie weights, uncooked beans, raw rice, pennies, or granulated sugar, keeping the decorated edges free of the weights.

Bake with the weights for 10 minutes, until pale golden on the edges.

Carefully remove the paper holding the weights and pop the pan back in the oven to dry out the crust, about 10 more minutes.

Cool the crust in the pan on a rack. It may be baked a few hours, or even a day, in advance and kept covered on the counter, awaiting filling. Do not refrigerate.

Increase the oven temperature to 425°F. Remove and discard the ribs from the kale and slice the leaves into thin ribbons. Place 1 cup in a small bowl and set aside.

Warm the butter in a straight-sided skillet over medium-high heat until foamy. Add the shallot and cook until wilted, just a minute or two. Add the remaining kale leaves, cover, reduce the heat to medium, and wilt the leaves for about 3 minutes. Remove the cover, add the crème fraîche, and stir until creamy and smooth, cooking only a minute or two so it remains saucy. Remove from the heat and add the smoked paprika. Set aside to cool slightly.

Spoon the olive oil over the reserved 1 cup raw kale and use your fingers to massage it into the leaves. Add more only if the leaves still seem dry.

Spread the creamy kale on the blind-baked crust. Top with the raw kale, pat it down and using the back of a tablespoon, form four wells in which to place the proscuitto. Form four cup shapes with the prosciutto slices and snuggle them into the kale. Carefully and quickly crack an egg into each prosciutto nest and pour a tablespoon of cream over each egg. Top with a sprinkle of hazelnuts and Parmigiano Reggiano.

Bake in the center of the oven for 15 to 18 minutes, until the egg whites no longer appear watery and the yolk is still runny, with crispy shards of kale everywhere.

Cut into 4 portions and serve up right away.

BANH MI-STYLE CARAMEL PORK TART

Serves 6

---

1 recipe All-Butter
Pie Dough, page
251, formed into
a 3- by 4-inch
rectangular block

Egg wash
(1 egg beaten
with 1 tablespoon
cool water and
¼ teaspoon
kosher salt)

---

3 tablespoons
grapeseed or
canola oil

1 pound (450 g)
pork tenderloin,
trimmed of silver
skin

¼ cup (28 g)
diced shallots

1 teaspoon
minced garlic

1 teaspoon grated
fresh ginger

3 tablespoons
packed brown
sugar

3 tablespoons
fish sauce

2 tablespoons
soy sauce

½ teaspoon
sesame oil

½ cup (85 g)
Chicken Liver
Terrine (recipe
follows), optional

2 tablespoons
crème fraîche or
mayonnaise

½ to 1 teaspoon
Sriracha hot
sauce, to your
taste

½ cup (85 g)
Pickled Carrot and
Daikon (recipe
follows)

¼ cup (15 g)
chopped cilantro
leaves and stems

¼ cup (15 g)
chopped fresh
mint leaves

¼ cup (15 g)
julienned (rolled
up like a cigar and
sliced in ribbons)
fresh Thai or
Italian basil

A few thin slices
fresh jalapeño
(optional)

For me, banh mi, the Vietnamese sandwich, is all about crisp pickles, warm tangy saucy pork, and the umami of chicken livers. The pickles are easy to stir together and essential to the whole gestalt of banh mi, so make them. The chicken liver terrine, while optional, adds so substantially to the complexity that I hope you'll make it or buy a duck or chicken liver pâté to use in its place. The sauce for the pork mimics the quintessentially Vietnamese savory caramel—sweet, salty, bright, and sumptuous. This beautiful tart is best when assembled and served warm—the freshly cooked, highly scented, thinly sliced pork piled atop a fully baked crust, garnished with bright pickles and a shower of fresh herbs.

Line a baking sheet with parchment. Lightly dust the counter with flour and roll the dough into a generous 11-inch square. Trim and tidy to 10 inches square with a paring knife, pizza wheel, or decorative pastry wheel. Lift the dough using a bench scraper or offset spatula, roll over the pin or fold gently, and briskly transfer to the baking sheet; be brave and adjust the shape as needed after moving.

From the dough trimmings, trim or cut out forms to make a decorative edge (see page 96). Brush with egg wash and stack along the edges of the square. Pay particular attention to the corners. Pierce the dough all over with a fork or docking tool. Brush the edges with egg wash. Chill the dough for 20 to 30 minutes.

Place a Baking Steel, baking stone, or inverted baking sheet on the center rack and heat the oven to 375°F.

Cut a piece of foil or parchment paper slightly larger than

(Continued)

---

the size of the dough and spray one side with cooking spray. Place it on top of the unbaked crust, the sprayed side facing down. Make sure there is enough paper overhanging the edges of the dough for easy lifting later. Fill generously with pie weights, uncooked beans, raw rice, pennies, or granulated sugar, keeping the decorated edges free of the weights.

Bake with the weights for 20 minutes, until golden brown and crisp on the edges.

Carefully remove the paper holding the weights and pop the pastry back in the oven to dry out the crust, about 10 more minutes.

Cool the crust in the pan on a rack. It may be baked a few hours, or even a day, in advance and kept covered on the counter, awaiting filling. Do not refrigerate.

Increase the oven temperature to 400°F. Heat 1 tablespoon of the oil in a heavy, oven-proof skillet over high heat. When it shimmers, lower the tenderloin into the pan. It should sizzle. Let the meat brown and do not mess with it. When it releases easily, after about 4 minutes, turn and continue to brown the other side until it easily releases from the pan, another 4 or 5 minutes. Slide the pan into the oven and continue to cook the tenderloin until the internal temperature reaches 140°F, 10 to 15 minutes. Remove from the oven and let it rest for 10 minutes, loosely tented with foil.

While the pork rests, make the sauce. Heat the remaining 2 tablespoons oil in a medium skillet over medium-high heat until shimmering. Add the shallots and cook for 2 or 3 minutes, then stir in the garlic and ginger and cook for another minute. Add the brown sugar, fish sauce, soy sauce, and sesame oil. Bring to a boil and cook until reduced by one-quarter, about 6 minutes. Slice the pork into ⅛-inch slices and toss with the sauce to coat. Remove from the heat.

Spread the chicken liver terrine, if using, across the tart. Combine the crème fraîche and Sriracha in a small bowl. Use an offset spatula to spread the spicy mayonnaise across the tart. Pile the saucy pork slices on top. Top with pickles, chopped herbs, and jalapeños (if using). Use a serrated knife or a pizza wheel to slice the tart into six pieces and serve immediately.

PICKLED CARROT AND DAIKON

Makes about 2 cups

1 medium carrot

½ medium daikon

½ cup (120 ml) rice wine vinegar

¼ cup (60 ml) water

1 tablespoon granulated sugar

1½ teaspoons kosher salt

The classic banh mi sandwich is filled with rich, unctuous meats and offset by bright, crunchy pickles. These pickles will keep in the refrigerator for a month or more, but I like them best in the first day or two after they're made, when still very snappy. If a daikon is not available, substitute big, fat, red radishes, sliced into thin disks.

Peel and slice the carrot and daikon into slim matchsticks. (A mandoline is very useful here, but please be careful of your fingers.) Stuff the carrot and daikon into a pint-sized jar with a lid. In a small saucepan, bring the vinegar, water, sugar, and salt to a boil. Remove from the heat and pour over the carrots and daikon. Let the mixture cool on the counter, cover, and refrigerate. The pickles are ready to eat in an hour, but can be made up to 2 weeks in advance.

CHICKEN LIVER TERRINE

Makes 2 cups, packed (450 g)

1 (¼-ounce) packet powdered unflavored gelatin, about 2¼ to 2½ teaspoons

½ cup (120 ml) boiling water

8 tablespoons (113 g) unsalted butter, softened

½ pound (225 g) fresh chicken livers, cleaned, patted dry, sinews removed

1 teaspoon minced shallot

1 Granny Smith apple, peeled, cored, and chopped (about 1 cup)

3 tablespoons cognac or Armagnac

1½ teaspoons kosher salt

½ teaspoon freshly ground black pepper

¼ teaspoon Dijon mustard

¼ teaspoon allspice

I'm a sucker for a great liver terrine and this one fits the bill. I make it in batches, freeze in small ramekins, and always have a rich, guilty pleasure ready to be defrosted. I like it scented with Armagnac to remind me of Gascony, one of my favorite places. This delicious terrine adds a distinct texture and liquor-scented flavor to the banh mi tart, and you'll have enough left over to squirrel away for a rainy day. I pack and freeze in 4-ounce ramekins. Cornichons are a classic, necessary, condiment.

Have ready four 4-ounce ramekins or other dishes suitable for serving. In a small bowl, sprinkle the gelatin over the boiling water, stir, and set aside.

Heat about 1 tablespoon of the butter in a large nonstick skillet over medium-high heat. When melted and frothy, add the livers and cook until the exterior is slightly browned, about 8 minutes. Reduce the heat to medium, add the shallot and apple, and cook until softened, 8 to 9 minutes. There should be no pink remaining in the liver.

Scoop the livers and apple into the work bowl of a food processor and puree while still hot. Add the gelatin mixture and continue to run the processor until it is completely smooth. Add the cognac, salt, pepper, mustard, and allspice and process again until smooth.

Let the mixture cool in the food processor work bowl, uncovered, until cool to the touch, about 15 minutes. You will be adding butter, but you do not want the butter to melt in—rather, it's better for the butter to be beaten in, emulsifying the terrine. Return the cover to the work bowl, and with the processor running, add the remaining 7 tablespoons butter a few bits at a time, processing after each by pulsing the mixture until smooth. After all the butter has been incorporated, stir the mixture well and pour into the ramekins. Cover well and chill overnight to allow the terrine to set and the flavors to develop. If freezing, cover tightly and place in the freezer as soon as the mixture has cooled.

This sensational umami-bomb may be made well in advance. It will keep in the refrigerator for 3 days and in the freezer for 3 months. Defrost overnight in the refrigerator.

SAVORY NECTARINE MASCARPONE TART

Serves 8

---

1 recipe All-Butter Pie Dough, page 251, formed into a disk

Egg wash (1 egg beaten with 1 tablespoon cool water and ¼ teaspoon kosher salt)

---

2 tablespoons (28 g) unsalted butter

⅓ fennel bulb, thinly sliced into half-moons (½ cup, 70 g)

½ small red onion, thinly sliced into half-moons (¼ cup, 35 g)

3 barely ripe nectarines, thickly sliced (2 cups, 355 g)

1 teaspoon fresh lime juice

Generous ¼ cup (56 g) mascarpone, at room temperature

1 tablespoon finely minced fresh mint

1 tablespoon honey

¼ cup (35 g) toasted hazelnuts, chopped

The first glimmerings of an idea for fruit tart as an appetizer germinated in 2009 when a cook named Jackie posted a terrific plum tart on Food52. Soon, I was riffing on the idea in all sorts of directions, using roasted pineapple, wilted plums, deeply jammy sweet cherries, grape halves, and sugar-fried banana, all with different creamy spreads and cheeses, all sorts of drizzles, the spike of acid, and always with soft, wilted onions. After so many delicious versions, this became my go-to favorite.

Line a baking sheet with parchment. Lightly dust the counter with flour and roll the dough into an approximate 12-inch round. Trim and tidy the shape to about 11 inches with a paring knife, pizza wheel, or decorative pastry wheel. Lift the dough using a bench scraper or offset spatula and briskly transfer to the baking sheet; be brave and adjust the shape as needed after moving.

Turn about an inch of the dough edge toward the center, then pinch and crimp so the final size is about 9 inches across. Pierce the dough all over with a fork or docking tool. Brush the edges with egg wash. Chill for 20 to 30 minutes.

Place a Baking Steel, baking stone, or inverted baking sheet on the center rack and heat the oven to 375°F.

Cut a piece of foil or parchment paper slightly larger than the size of the dough and spray one side with cooking spray. Lay it on top of the unbaked crust with the sprayed side facing down. Make sure there is enough paper overhanging the edges of the dough for easy lifting later. Fill generously with pie weights, uncooked beans, raw rice, pennies, or

(Continued)

granulated sugar, keeping the decorated edges free of the weights.

Bake with the weights for 20 minutes, until golden brown and crisp on the edges.

Carefully remove the paper holding the weights and pop the pastry back in the oven to dry out the crust, about 10 more minutes.

Cool the crust in the pan on a rack. It may be baked a few hours, or even a day, in advance and kept covered on the counter, awaiting filling. Do not refrigerate.

Melt the butter over medium-high heat in a large, wide, nonstick skillet until melted and foaming. Add the fennel and onion and cook until wilted and slightly golden at the edges. Transfer to a small bowl using a slotted spoon. Add the nectarines to the pan and cook, tossing them in the remaining butter until softened and slightly caramelized on the edges, about 5 or 6 minutes. Splash the lime juice across the surface of the nectarines. Remove the pan from the heat and cool for 10 minutes or so.

Assemble the tart: Spread the mascarpone across the base of the tart, avoiding the edges. Spoon the wilted onion and fennel across the tart, then place the nectarines decoratively across the surface. Garnish with the mint, squiggle the honey on top, and scatter the nuts across the surface. Serve immediately.

STRAWBERRY JAM TART WITH TOASTED STREUSEL

Serves 8

1 recipe Cream Cheese Pie Dough, page 252, formed into a square block

Egg wash (1 egg beaten with 1 tablespoon cool water and ¼ teaspoon kosher salt)

⅓ cup (40 g) all-purpose flour

⅓ cup (37 g) slivered almonds, chopped

¼ cup (25 g) rolled (not instant) oats

2 tablespoons packed brown sugar

⅛ teaspoon ground cinnamon

Large pinch kosher salt

2 tablespoons (28 g) unsalted butter, cubed and chilled

8 ounces (225 g) strawberry jam (1 scant cup)

A lmost a cookie, it's only the crust that keeps this delightful treat firmly in the pie category. There are few ingredients here, so make sure the jam is particularly delicious. While I call for strawberry, use any jam that you love, any flavor. If you make your own, this is a worthy showcase. The jam should be stiff, not runny, or it will spill out of the crust. Slice this slim, crisp tart into squares to serve with ice cream.

Line a baking sheet with parchment. Lightly dust the counter with flour and roll the dough into a generous 11-inch square. Trim and tidy to 9 inches square with a paring knife, pizza wheel, or decorative pastry wheel. Lift the dough using a bench scraper or offset spatula and briskly transfer it to the baking sheet; be brave and adjust the shape as needed after moving.

Using the trimmed dough, cut out forms or long strips to make a decorative edge (see page 96). Use egg wash as the glue to stack the cutouts on the pastry, paying particular attention to making highly adorned corners. Stack cutout on cutout and make sure they touch all along the edge, a wall to hold back the extravagant jam. Pierce the dough all over with a fork or a docking tool. Brush the edges with egg wash. Chill for 20 to 30 minutes.

Place a Baking Steel, baking stone, or inverted baking sheet on the center rack and heat the oven to 375°F.

Cut a piece of foil or parchment paper slightly larger than the size of the dough and spray one side with cooking spray. Lay it on top of the unbaked crust with the sprayed side facing down. Make sure there is enough paper overhanging the edges of the dough for easy lifting later. Fill generously with

pie weights, uncooked beans, raw rice, pennies, or granulated sugar, keeping the decorated edges free of the weights.

Bake with the weights for 10 minutes, until golden brown and crisp on the edges.

Carefully remove the paper holding the weights and pop the pastry back in the oven to dry out the crust, about 10 more minutes.

Reduce the oven temperature to 350°F.

Cool the crust in the pan on a rack. It may be baked a few hours, or even a day, in advance and kept covered on the counter, awaiting filling. Do not refrigerate.

While the crust is baking, line a baking sheet with parchment. Add the flour, almonds, oats, brown sugar, cinnamon, and salt and stir it around. Bake until slightly toasty, about 10 minutes. Scrape the streusel onto a plate to cool, about 10 minutes. Pinch in the chilled butter until gravelly and deliciously scented.

Spread the still-warm crust with the jam and sprinkle the toasted streusel generously over the surface of the jam. You may not need all of it. (Save the remainder to sprinkle over a roasted peach—a little personal cobbler, just for you.) Bake the tart an additional 8 to 10 minutes, until the jam is bubbling under the golden brown streusel. Serve warm or at room temperature.

SOUR CHERRY STUFFED-CRUST TART

Serves 8

3 cups (300 g) fresh sour pie cherries, pitted over a bowl to capture all the juices

½ cup (100 g) granulated sugar

¼ cup (28 g) cornstarch

1 tablespoon freshly squeezed lemon juice

⅛ teaspoon kosher salt

⅛ teaspoon almond extract

2 recipes All-Butter Pie Dough, page 251, each formed into a disk

2 tablespoons (28 g) unsalted butter

Egg wash (1 egg beaten with 1 tablespoon cool water and ¼ teaspoon kosher salt)

3 tablespoons sparkling or turbinado sugar

Sour cherry is my pie. It's the pie I crave when I think of pie. When I was traveling and came upon some cherries in the market, I devised this self-contained tart, the very first of my flying pies. Playing with an idea I encountered at The Inn at Little Washington, the crust is stuffed with plump cherries. It's a cherry extravaganza. The cherries make a pastry wall that holds back the flood of filling. It's a tart that depends on a good hard freeze to retain its shape through the high heat of cooking. Even with a freeze, the round shape is likely to morph into more of an oval by the time it exits the oven. I've been known to make a lattice to bind the edges together with ropes of dough, but still the tart emerges more elliptical than round. No doubt an aeronautical engineer could tell me why.

Set aside about 20—⅓ cup (30 g)—of the pitted cherries to stuff the crust. Stir together the sugar, cornstarch, lemon juice, and salt in a medium saucepan. Add the remaining cherries and any accumulated juices to the pan and cook over high heat, stirring all the time, until boiling, about 7 minutes. Boil for exactly 1 minute, then remove from the heat; the filling will be thick and stiff. Stir in the almond extract and cool the filling. The filling may be refrigerated for up to 3 days.

Line two baking sheets with parchment. Remove one dough disk from the refrigerator, lightly dust the counter with flour, and roll the dough into a 10-inch round. Lift the dough using a bench scraper or offset spatula and briskly transfer to the baking sheet; be brave and adjust the shape as needed after moving. Trim to 9 inches across, with a clean, pretty edge.

(Continued)

On top of the pie dough, line up the reserved cherries in a circle, about ¼ inch apart and ½ inch in from the dough's edge. Lift and roll the dough's outside edge inward, up and over the cherries. Use your index finger to pinch and crimp between each cherry. If there are cherries left over, stir them into the filling. Cover and freeze the stuffed crust for 30 minutes.

Roll the second dough disc into an approximate 10-inch round. Use a small cookie cutter to stamp out 1-inch hearts, stars, or flowers. Place these cutouts on the other baking sheet, cover, and refrigerate or freeze for 20 minutes.

Place a Baking Steel, baking stone, or inverted baking sheet on the center rack and heat the oven to 400°F.

Pile the cherry filling into the center of the stuffed crust. Spread it out with an offset spatula until it just touches the edge. Dot the butter across the surface. Brush the cutouts with egg wash and place them across the surface of the tart. You can make the tart up to this point and freeze for several hours in advance.

Sprinkle the whole surface generously with sparkling sugar and slide the baking sheet into the oven. Bake until the crust is golden brown and the filling is bubbling, 30 to 40 minutes, whether frozen or not.

Cool for an hour, minimum, before serving.

GLAZED FRUIT TART

Serves 6 to 8

---

1 recipe All-Butter Pie Dough, page 251, formed into a 3- by 4-inch rectangular block

Egg wash (1 egg beaten with 1 tablespoon cool water and ¼ teaspoon kosher salt)

Pastry Cream (recipe follows)

2 cups beautiful fruit, sliced when appropriate—figs, raspberries, strawberries, blueberries, blackberries, peaches, nectarines, plums

About 2 tablespoons apricot jam, passed through a sieve to remove the pieces of fruit, or currant jelly for glazing, warmed

My mother was the Queen of Tarts. For years, pie was her thing, but at some moment she decided tarts were more fun. For her birthday, she would spell her name in blueberries across the pastry cream. She wished friends *Bon Voyage* on a tart shaped like an airplane (see Make a Stencil, page 98). She had fun with her tarts. A classic tart is a good recipe to have in your back pocket all summer. It's surprisingly straightforward for such a fancy thing and can be made tiny and precious, or vast and dramatic for large gatherings. The skills needed are dough rolling and custard making, neither of which is hard, but each improves with practice. In my mind's eye, my mother is forever pushing backward through the screen door, then spinning around, a fanciful tart in her hands.

Line a baking sheet with parchment. Heat the oven to 375°F. Lightly dust the counter with flour and roll the dough to an approximate 10- by 8-inch rectangle. Place on the baking sheet and turn the edge toward the center about 1 inch to form a thicker border. Decoratively crimp or otherwise fancy up the edge (see Layering, page 96). Pierce the dough all over with a fork or a docking tool. Brush the edges with egg wash.

Cut a piece of foil or parchment paper slightly larger than the size of the dough and spray one side with cooking spray. Lay it on top of the unbaked crust with the sprayed side facing down. Make sure there is enough paper overhanging the edges of the dough for easy lifting later. Fill generously with pie weights, uncooked beans, raw rice, pennies, or granulated sugar, keeping the decorated edges free of the weights.

Bake for 20 minutes, until golden brown and crisp on the edges.

(Continued)

Carefully remove the paper holding the weights and pop the pastry back in the oven to dry out the crust, about 10 more minutes.

Cool the crust in the pan on a rack. The crust may be baked several hours or even a day in advance and kept loosely covered on the counter, awaiting filling.

Spread the cold pastry cream thickly across the bottom of the tart shell. Decoratively place fruits across the surface. With a small pastry brush, paint the fruits carefully with the warmed jam to make them shine. Serve with pride, right away. (If you must, chill the tart for no more than an hour or the fruit will begin to weep.)

VARIATIONS

BIGGER. Make a double batch of pie dough and roll out a big tart base (16 by 12 inches). Trim to 15 by 10 inches with fancy edges and decorated corners and blind bake. You'll need a double batch of pastry cream and 4 cups of fruit.

SMALLER. Make 12 tiny tartlettes just 2½ inches across that will hold 2 tablespoons pastry cream and 3 to 5 blueberries. They're adorable.

LIGHTER. Combine the pastry cream with an equal amount of sturdy whipped cream for a fluffy, lightened filling, not quite as eggy. This filling will not keep and the fruit will weep very quickly, so the tart should be assembled and served immediately.

FRUITLESS. Use Coffee Pastry Cream (page 62) and scatter toffee bits and chopped chocolate across the surface.

PASTRY CREAM

Makes 1 ½ cups

1½ cups (360 ml) whole milk

3 tablespoons cornstarch

1 tablespoon all-purpose flour

3 large egg yolks, lightly beaten

¼ cup (50 g) granulated sugar

⅛ teaspoon kosher salt

2 tablespoons (28 g) unsalted butter, cubed

½ teaspoon vanilla extract

Pastry cream is rich and velvety. It's the eggy, creamy base for fruit tarts and tartlettes and makes insanely delicious treats (such as Fresh Apricot Breakfast Pastry, page 163). Below is a classic vanilla cream, but ¼ teaspoon almond extract may be swapped in for the vanilla extract. Or stir in 1 teaspoon rum, cognac, bourbon, kirsh, or orange liqueur to take the flavor in an adult direction.

Set a strainer over a bowl placed inside an ice bath.

In a small mixing bowl, whisk ½ cup of the milk with the cornstarch, flour, and egg yolks and set aside.

Combine the remaining 1 cup milk with the sugar and salt in a medium saucepan over medium-high heat. Let the mixture warm, stirring all the time as the sugar dissolves, about 4 minutes, until small bubbles appear at the edges.

Slowly whisk ¼ cup of the warm milk mixture into the egg yolk mixture. This process is called tempering and will keep the yolks from scrambling.

Pour the egg-milk mixture back into the warm milk in the pan, whisking the whole time. The next step should take about 5 minutes. Return the pan to medium-high heat, bring the mixture to a boil, and cook, constantly whisking, until the mixture thickens into a smooth sauce. This transformation will happen very suddenly, so stay vigilant; the pastry cream will be thick like custard or warm pudding.

Remove the pan from the heat and use the whisk or a sturdy spoon to push the custard through the strainer into the bowl set over the ice bath, removing any lumps. Stir in the butter cubes and vanilla extract and continue to stir until the pastry cream has cooled.

Cover with plastic wrap touching the surface of the custard to keep a skin from forming. Refrigerate for 2 hours, or until entirely cool. The custard will keep 3 days, but it's best when fresh. Custard does not freeze well.

MILLIONAIRE'S TART

Serves 8 to 10

---

1 recipe Brown-Butter Pie Dough, page 254, formed into a disk

Egg wash (1 egg beaten with 1 tablespoon cool water and ¼ teaspoon kosher salt)

CARAMEL

⅔ cup (160 ml) sweetened condensed milk

¼ cup (53 g) packed brown sugar

3 tablespoons (42 g) unsalted butter

1 tablespoon light corn syrup or golden syrup

½ teaspoon vanilla extract

⅛ teaspoon kosher salt

CHOCOLATE

6 ounces (170 g) bittersweet chocolate, chopped

3 tablespoons heavy cream

MERINGUE

3 egg whites (90 g), at room temperature

¼ teaspoon cream of tartar

½ cup (100 g) granulated sugar

¼ teaspoon vanilla extract

Caramel. Chocolate. Meringue. It's Millionaire's Short-bread, reimagined as a tart. I dreamed up this rich, pretty tart and couldn't wait until it was on my fork. It's decadent as can be and feels like a love letter of a pie, so I made it heart shaped and added the meringue in big swirls until it was as over the top as possible. Small slices will suffice.

Make a 9-inch heart-shaped stencil (see page 98) or draw a heart freehand on a piece of parchment paper and trim the paper to form. Line a baking sheet with foil. Lightly dust the counter with flour and roll the dough into a generous 10-inch round that is about ⅛ inch thick. Using the stencil, cut out the heart shape and transfer to the lined baking sheet. (Step 1.)

Brush the edge of the dough with the egg wash. Pierce the dough all over with a fork or docking tool. Use the trimmings to cut out several additional hearts and flowers of various sizes and stack them all along the edge of the heart base. Brush the cutouts with egg wash. Chill the dough for 20 to 30 minutes.

Place a Baking Steel, baking stone, or inverted baking sheet on the center rack and heat the oven to 375°F.

Cut a piece of foil or parchment paper slightly larger than the size of the dough and spray one side with cooking spray. Lay it on top of the unbaked crust with the sprayed side facing down. Make sure there is enough paper overhanging the edges of the dough for easy lifting later. Fill generously with pie weights, uncooked beans, raw rice, pennies, or granulated sugar, keeping the decorated edges free of the weights. (Step 2.)

Bake with the weights for 10 minutes, until golden brown and crisp on the edges.

(Continued)

Carefully remove the paper holding the weights and pop the pastry back in the oven to dry out the crust, about 10 more minutes.

Cool the crust in the pan on a rack. It may be baked a few hours, or even a day, in advance and kept covered on the counter, awaiting filling. Do not refrigerate.

FOR THE CARAMEL: While the crust is baking, in a small saucepan over medium heat, combine the condensed milk, brown sugar, butter, corn syrup, vanilla, and salt. Bring to a low simmer and cook, stirring all the time, until reduced and thick as yogurt. This will take about 10 minutes. It will be pale tan, not deep brown. Remove from the heat.

FOR THE CHOCOLATE: While the crust is baking, bring 2 inches of water to a boil in a medium saucepan over high heat. Reduce the heat until the water is just simmering, not at a brisk boil. Top the saucepan with a heatproof glass or metal bowl that sits above the water. Add the chopped chocolate and cream to the bowl and stir until it is thick, melted, and spreadable. Remove the pan from the heat and the bowl from the pan; but keep the warm water in the pan to rewarm the chocolate, if needed.

FOR THE MERINGUE: In the bowl of a stand mixer, beat the egg whites with the whisk attachment on high until good and foamy. Add the cream of tartar and continue to beat on high, until the whites turn opaque. Begin to slowly add the sugar, 1 tablespoon at a time, while the mixer continues to run. When all the sugar has been added, stop the mixer and lift the beater. You're looking for a stiff peak, a very lofty meringue that stands up on its own. Once it's reached peaky perfection, add the vanilla and beat to combine. If you're feeling fancy, spoon the meringue into a piping bag fitted with a decorative tip, or leave in the bowl to simply scoop the meringue from the mixing bowl onto the tart.

Now you're ready to assemble the tart. Place an oven rack in the upper part of the oven, about 6 inches from the broiler element, keeping in mind the meringue topping will be quite tall, as much as 3 inches off the baking sheet. Turn the oven to broil.

Spoon the still warm caramel over the crust, avoiding the edges. It should be thick and spreadable and sct up almost instantly. Add the chocolate gently, spreading it across the caramel with an offset spatula and keeping the layers distinct. (Step 3.) Add the meringue either by piping it or by scooping up a big spoonful and plopping it across the surface, using the back of a big round spoon to make fluffy clouds from edge to edge. (Step 4.)

Pop the tart under the broiler for 2 to 5 minutes. Do not take your eyes off this beauty and wait for the unmistakable scent of toasting marshmallows. Yes, you can let some of the tips of the meringue mountains blacken very slightly, but then quickly get that tart out of the oven before it's ruined.

Let the tart sit for a minute or two and then dive in. Slice the heart in half and then in wedges up each side. Wait for the *Mmmmm* sounds.

CHAPTER 5

STRUDEL, PUFF, AND PHYLLO

WRAP-AROUNDS FROM EUROPE AND THE MIDDLE EAST

Here are pie-adjacent pastries, where dough wraps around a filling. We start with strudel, a whisper-thin, stretchy dough that is filled, rolled, and baked. Puff pastry is layer upon layer of dough separated by leaves of butter, a rich pastry to hug any filling. And phyllo, the papery dough swabbed with butter, makes cheese-filled appetizers fit for company.

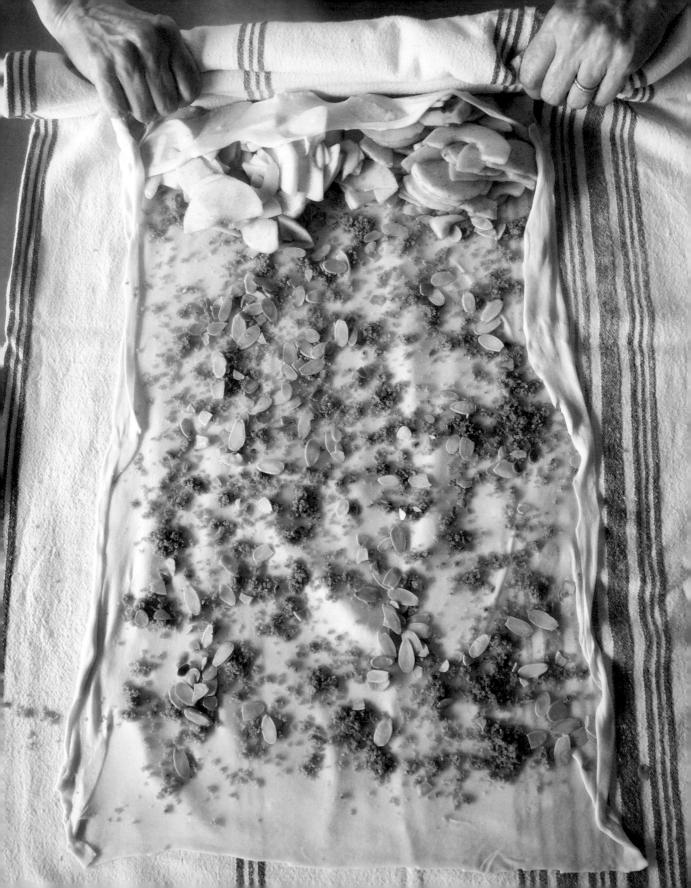

STRUDEL
FLAKY, WISPY LAYERS

Strudel dough is highly elastic with well-developed gluten. It isn't rolled, but stretched until paper thin, usually atop a soft, flour-dusted cloth. When I read recipes for strudel, many referenced pulling the dough so thin the design on the cloth below was evident. As I learned the technique, I envisioned generations of strudel makers gathering around a table to pull and fill, roll and tuck, forming stuffed cylinders of flaky layers. Like so many other forms in this book, savory strudel is a common way to feed more with less, devising fillings that are rich, complex, and satisfying. Fruit strudels—apple being the most ubiquitous—are a pie in another form, where the fruit flavor is enhanced by the pastry, but never overwhelmed.

Make the Pulled Dough for Strudel (page 262) the night before and let it relax and chill thoroughly in the refrigerator. About an hour before starting to stretch it, take out the dough, but do not unwrap it (it will dry out).

Be prepared, ready to roll, and strudel becomes a weeknight dinner solution. This is the time for a restaurant-worthy *mis en place*. Have your chilled filling ingredients ready to go, as well as the melted butter and the bread crumbs. Prepare the baking sheet.

When ready, lift the dough by one edge so it falls away and stretches out all by itself. If it's flexible, you're ready to stretch. If not, cover and let it rest another 10 minutes then try again. Cold dough will not stretch.

The entire act of stretching the dough and then filling and rolling the strudel should take about 10 minutes. Don't sweat it. It's a home cook's pastry, this strudel idea, and should not fill you with fear. Sure, your first strudel will be a little lumpy and there may be some holes, but it's going to work out, taste great, and with some

practice every subsequent strudel will be more consistent and snugly formed. It's certainly possible to stretch a sheet of strudel dough all by yourself, but with a friend (or a willing child) helping, it's so much more fun.

STRETCHING THE DOUGH

Set up the strudel stretching table or countertop with a linen or cotton cloth, tablecloth, or an extra-large cotton tea towel. The final size of the pulled dough will be about 20 by 24 inches and the cloth should be larger by at least 2 inches all the way around.

Flour the cloth heavily, using the heel of your hand to rub the flour into the surface of the cloth. Brush away any excess. Remove the strudel dough from the ziptop bag and with floured hands, place it on the towel, turn it to get some flour on each side. Lift the dough and let it fall away, turning it so it stretches from the edge. Next, use a rolling pin to roll the dough to about 10 by 10 inches. Now lift the dough and with your hands forming fists and thumbs tucked in (and rings off!), let the edge of the dough ride your knuckles while also slowly spinning it, so the weight of the dough itself causes it to stretch. Imagine you are making pizza in the window of a pizzeria, because it's the same action. Use the weight of the dough to stretch it, and then knuckles and fingertips to tap and pull and lightly, gently expand the dough to a rectangle thin as air.

Once the dough is about 16 by 16 inches, place it down on the floured towel and continue to stretch, placing one hand lightly on the surface of the dough, and working with the other hand from the underside, the knuckles of your loose fist stretching the dough to the edge to get to the 20- by 24-inch goal. You'll see the dough become

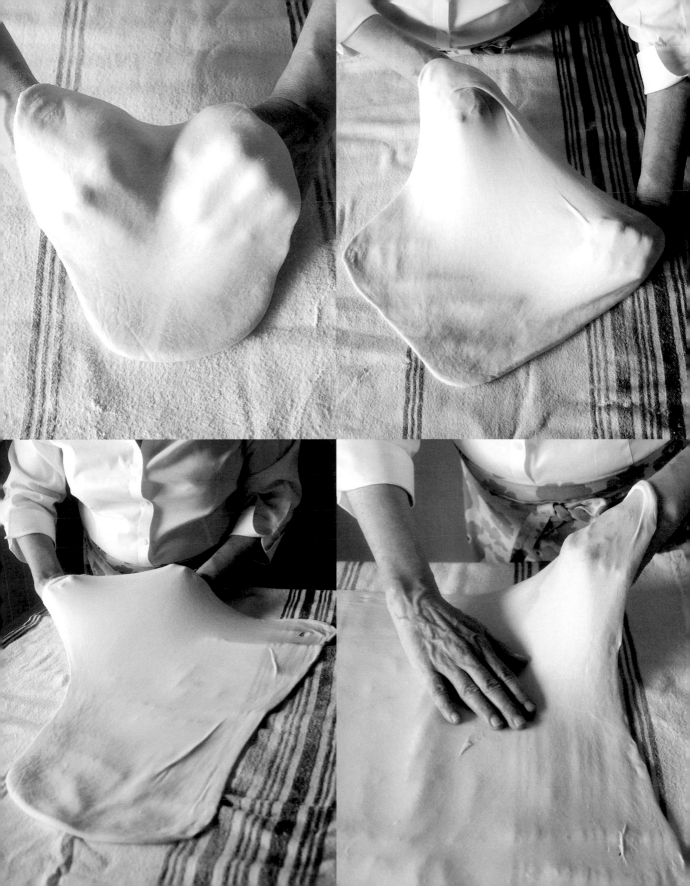

increasingly translucent. You may get a hole here and there. Just move away from that area and move to another spot that needs thinning. Once the strudel is rolled, those holes won't matter. This whole process doesn't take long at all, just 5 minutes or so, once you've done it a few times. Pull the dough until it's possible to "read a newspaper through it" or some close approximation of that idea.

Pat it into shape, take a breath, and, using scissors or your fingertips, tear or cut away the thick edges and discard. Proceed with the recipe, filling, rolling, and baking the strudel. Do not let the dough sit out once it's been stretched as it will dry out and then won't roll well at all. And remember: Have all your ingredients ready to go before beginning to strudel.

ROLLING THE STRUDEL

Form the filling into a tidy, firm log on the stretched strudel dough along a 20-inch side, about 2 inches from the edge. Yes, a log shape will be more challenging with sliced apples, but do your best. Lift and pull the bare 2-inch edge of the dough over the filling and tuck in the sides, as you might when making a burrito. Use the strudel cloth to lift and roll the dough, pressing lightly to form a tight log. The goal is to make this log firm and tight, not loose and sloppy. Your first strudel will look humble. Your third will look fantastic.

Transfer the strudel in the cloth and tip it onto a parchment-lined baking sheet with the seam side down. Butter it well, get that strudel in the oven, and congratulate yourself.

SLICING AND SAUCING

Let the strudel cool for about 10 minutes after baking before trying to slice it. This will give the filling time to settle and the pastry a minute to firm up. I can't decide if I prefer slicing strudel with a very sharp chef's knife or a serrated bread knife—both work well.

Savory strudel is delicious with any sauce that complements the filling. Think of the strudel as re-imagining your leftovers, so gravy or cheese sauce or any sort of pan sauce fits right in. Put a puddle on the plate and snuggle in a slab of strudel—suddenly, tonight's dinner looks fancy and not at all like last night's meal.

Sweet strudels can also get dressed up with a good sauce. When fruit macerates even for just a few minutes, it will be far too wet to make a strudel filling. So when you are making the filling, strain the fruit well (see Another Kind of Apple Sauce, at the Spiced Apple Strudel recipe, page 152), then reduce the leftover liquids to a syrup-y, flavor bomb of a delicious sauce. Every sweet strudel shines under a dollop of whipped cream or a scoop of ice cream. Only the best for your homemade strudel.

KALE, MUSHROOM, AND GRUYÈRE STRUDEL

Serves 8 to 10

1 recipe Pulled Dough for Strudel, page 262

2 tablespoons olive oil

8 ounces (225 g) cremini mushrooms, stemmed and sliced ¼ inch thick

1 medium onion, diced (about 1 cup, 142 g)

8 ounces (225 g) lacinato kale, ribs removed and leaves roughly chopped (about 3 cups)

¼ cup (15 g) chopped flat-leaf parsley

1 teaspoon fresh thyme leaves

1½ teaspoons kosher salt

¾ teaspoon freshly ground black pepper

1 large egg, beaten

6 ounces (170 g) Gruyère cheese, shredded

4 tablespoons (56 g) unsalted butter, melted

¼ cup (28 g) dry bread crumbs

A decadent and worthy way to get your veggies, this is a spectacular dish for buffets and potlucks, or served as a vegetarian side in a meat-heavy dinner (think Thanksgiving). The mushrooms are the star here and I rely on a pan-roasting technique for deep flavor and a texture that is never waterlogged. If you are a forager, or know one, using chanterelles or morels would be sublime.

Bring the strudel dough to room temperature for 1 hour before stretching, keeping it in the ziptop bag until ready to use. Heat the oven to 400°F and place a rack in the lower third of the oven. Line a baking sheet with parchment.

Heat the oil in a large heavy skillet over high heat. When the oil is shimmering, add the mushroom slices and reduce the heat to medium-high. Do not mess with the mushrooms. Let them pan-roast and get deeply browned, 6 to 8 minutes, before giving the pan a hard shake so they release. Then turn the mushrooms and roast for another 4 to 5 minutes, until well browned and crisped. Add the onion, stir well, and cook until wilted, 5 or 6 minutes. Add the chopped kale and cook for another 3 minutes, until the kale has collapsed but is still brightly colored. Stir in the parsley, thyme, salt, and pepper. Spread the mixture across a baking sheet to cool. (Freeze or refrigerate to speed the cooling process.) Once thoroughly cool, return to a bowl, and stir in the egg and cheese.

Prepare the work surface and stretch the strudel dough to 20 by 24 inches, until it's possible to "read a newspaper through it" or some close approximation of that idea (see page 138 for complete instructions). The whole process

doesn't take long at all, just 5 minutes or so, once you've done it a few times.

Pat the stretched dough into shape and then, using scissors or your fingertips, tear or cut away the thick edges and discard. Carefully swab the dough with about 2 tablespoons of the melted butter.

Add 1 tablespoon of the melted butter to the bread crumbs and stir well. Sprinkle the bread crumbs generously over the dough, leaving a 2-inch border. Transfer the kale filling to the dough using your hands and shape it into a log about 2 inches from a shorter edge.

Begin rolling by lifting and pulling the bare 2-inch edge of the dough over the kale log. Tuck in the sides and, using the strudel cloth, lift and roll the strudel into a tight log with the thin layers of strudel dough encasing the filling (see page 141). The goal is to make this log firm and tight, not loose and sloppy.

Use the cloth to transfer the strudel to the prepared baking sheet, seam side down.

Brush the top and sides of the strudel with the remaining melted butter. Bake for 20 to 25 minutes, until golden brown. Cool in the pan for 10 minutes before slicing and serving.

If serving later, reheat for a few minutes in a 350°F oven.

POTATO AND BACON STRUDEL

Serves 8 to 10

1 recipe Pulled Dough for Strudel, page 262

1½ pounds (680 g) Yukon Gold potatoes, peeled and cut into chunks

3½ ounces (100 g) thick-cut smoked bacon, diced

1 medium onion, sliced into half-moons (about 1 cup, 142 g)

½ cup (113 g) sour cream, full-fat yogurt, or crème fraîche

4 tablespoons (56 g) unsalted butter

2 tablespoons minced fresh chives

1½ teaspoons kosher salt

¾ teaspoon freshly ground black pepper

4 tablespoons (56 g) unsalted butter, melted

¼ cup (28 g) dry bread crumbs

*F*lammeküche is a magical pie brought forth from wood-burning ovens in Alsace, France. I traveled there and became so enamored of this flat pie that I ate one every day. It was the bacon. Or maybe it was the onion. Or it might have been the dough. But whatever it was, when I set out to make a strudel filling from mashed potatoes, it was *flammeküche's* smoky, bacony, oniony essence I most wanted to emulate. Make sure the filling is completely cool before stretching and filling the strudel.

Bring the strudel dough to room temperature for 1 hour before stretching, keeping it in the ziptop bag until ready to use. Heat the oven to 400°F and place a rack in the lower third of the oven. Line a baking sheet with parchment.

Place the potatoes in a medium saucepan and cover with cold water. Bring to a boil over high heat and cook until fork tender, 10 to 12 minutes. In the meantime, place the bacon in a small skillet and crisp over medium heat until cooked through but not dry, about 8 minutes. With a slotted spoon, transfer the bacon to a large bowl, leaving the bacon fat in the pan. Add the onion to the skillet and cook until golden on the edges, 5 or 6 minutes.

Drain the potatoes in a colander and then shake hard to release as much water as possible. Add the potatoes and the onions to the bowl with the bacon and, using a potato masher or a fork, smash the potatoes until pea-sized. Mash in the sour cream, butter, chives, salt, and pepper until mostly smooth. Spread the mixture across a baking sheet to cool. (Freeze or refrigerate to speed the cooling process.)

Prepare the work surface and stretch the strudel dough to 20 by 24 inches, until it's possible to "read a newspaper through it" or some close approximation of that idea (see

page 138 for complete instructions). The whole process doesn't take long at all, just 5 minutes or so, once you've done it a few times.

Pat the stretched dough into shape and then, using scissors or your fingertips, tear or cut away the thick edges and discard.

Add 1 tablespoon of the melted butter to the bread crumbs and stir well. Sprinkle generously over the dough, leaving a 2-inch border. Transfer the potato mixture to the dough using your hands and shape into a log about 2 inches from a short edge.

Begin rolling by lifting and pulling the bare 2-inch edge of the dough over the potato log. Tuck in the sides and, using the strudel cloth, lift and roll the strudel into a tight log with the thin layers of strudel dough encasing the filling (see page 141). The goal is to make this log firm and tight, not loose and sloppy.

Use the cloth to transfer the strudel to the prepared baking sheet, seam side down.

Brush the top and sides of the strudel with the remaining melted butter. Bake for 20 to 25 minutes, until golden brown. Cool in the pan for just 5 minutes before slicing and serving.

If serving later, reheat for a few minutes in a 350°F oven.

PEAR, SWEET POTATO, AND PISTACHIO STRUDEL

Serves 8 to 10

1 recipe Pulled Dough for Strudel, page 262

¼ cup (60 ml) port wine, Madeira, or red wine

10 prunes, pitted and chopped

1 pound (450 g) sweet potatoes, peeled (about 2 medium)

1 pound (450 g) slightly underripe Bosc or Bartlett pears (about 2 medium)

½ cup (60 g) pistachios, chopped

1 teaspoon grated orange zest

1 teaspoon ground ginger

½ teaspoon kosher salt

4 tablespoons (56 g) unsalted butter, melted

¼ cup (28 g) dry bread crumbs

½ cup (106 g) packed brown sugar

This strudel was inspired by memories of *tzimmes*, the irresistible combination of root vegetables and dried fruit served at many Jewish celebratory feasts. It's an adaptable recipe, so swap in butternut squash or carrots (but not the purple ones or risk an odd-looking strudel) for the sweet potatoes. By the same token, try dried apricots instead of the prunes—or maybe dried pears or golden raisins. It's the balance of sweet and savory that makes it special, and also causes one to wonder: Is this dinner or is this dessert? I say dessert, but you may feel otherwise. Make it even more savory by exchanging ½ cup crumbled blue cheese for the brown sugar.

Bring the strudel dough to room temperature for 1 hour before stretching, keeping it in the ziptop bag until ready to use. Heat the oven to 400°F and place a rack in the lower third of the oven. Line a baking sheet with parchment.

In a small saucepan, heat the port until warm but not boiling and remove from the heat. Add the prunes and let the fruit steep for 30 minutes. Transfer the prunes and port to a large bowl. Slice the sweet potatoes lengthwise in half and, using a mandoline or a very sharp knife and a sense of purpose, slice them very, very thin, ⅛ inch at most. Place them in the bowl with the prunes.

Peel and core the pear and thinly slice with the mandoline. Add the pear, pistachio, orange zest, ginger, and salt to the sweet potatoes and prunes and gently stir. I use my hands.

Prepare the work surface and stretch the strudel dough to 20 by 24 inches, until it's possible to "read a newspaper through it" or some close approximation of that idea (see

page 138 for complete instructions). The whole process doesn't take long at all, just 5 minutes or so, once you've done it a few times.

Pat the stretched dough into shape and then, using scissors or your fingertips, tear or cut away the thick edges and discard.

Add 1 tablespoon of the melted butter to the bread crumbs and stir well. Sprinkle generously over the dough, leaving a 2-inch border. Sprinkle brown sugar on top of the bread crumbs. Transfer the pear and potato filling to the dough, using your hands and leaving the liquid behind. Shape it into a log about 2 inches from a short edge.

Begin rolling by lifting and pulling the bare 2-inch edge of the dough over the log. Tuck in the sides and, using the strudel cloth, lift and roll the strudel into a tight log with the thin layers of strudel dough encasing the filling (see page 141). The goal is to make this log firm and tight, not loose and sloppy.

Use the cloth to transfer the strudel to the prepared baking sheet, seam side down.

Brush the top and sides of the strudel with the remaining melted butter. Bake for 20 to 25 minutes, until golden brown. Cool in the pan for 10 minutes before slicing and serving.

If serving later, reheat for a few minutes in a 350°F oven.

SPICED APPLE STRUDEL

Serves 8 to 10

1 recipe Pulled Dough for Strudel, page 262

4 tablespoons (55 g) unsalted butter

½ cup (60 g) dry bread crumbs

½ cup (43 g) sliced or slivered almonds

Juice of 1 lemon

1½ pounds (680 g) firm apples like Granny Smith, Pink Lady, or Pink Pearl

¾ cup (150 g) granulated sugar

3 tablespoons (45 ml) spiced dark rum

1 teaspoon ground cinnamon

¼ teaspoon freshly grated nutmeg

3 tablespoons (42 g) unsalted butter, melted

Powdered sugar for decorating

Apple strudel is a heavenly pastry to serve to a crowd. It smells like autumn should. Once the sugar hits the apples, they will begin to get juicy, which makes strudeling a little more challenging, so work quickly and with purpose. Feel free to omit the nuts, or substitute pecans or walnuts, according to your particular tastes. I like this just as much with firm, slightly underripe pears as I do with apples. Or try substituting quince for some or all of the apples for a heavenly, slightly pink delight.

Bring the strudel dough to room temperature for 1 hour before stretching, keeping it wrapped until ready to use so it will not dry out. Place the oven rack in the lower third of the oven. Heat the oven to 400°F and line a baking sheet with parchment.

In a large skillet, melt the butter over medium-high heat until foaming. Add the bread crumbs, stir well to coat with the butter, and toast until scented and golden, 1 to 2 minutes. Scrape the bread crumbs into a small bowl and wipe out the pan. Place the almonds in the pan, shaking and turning them over medium heat for 3 or 4 minutes, until slightly golden at the edges. Stir the almonds into the bread crumbs.

Juice the lemon into a large bowl. Peel the apples, slice in half, and core (I use a melon baller); then slice into half-moons no more than ⅛ inch thick. Add the apple slices to the bowl and gently stir around in the lemon juice so they will not brown. Add only ½ cup of the sugar, the rum, cinnamon, and nutmeg to the apples and gently stir together. I use my hands.

Prepare the work surface and stretch the strudel dough to 20 by 24 inches, until it's possible to "read a newspaper through it" or some close approximation of that idea (see

page 138 for complete instructions). The whole process doesn't take long at all, just 5 minutes or so, once you've done it a few times.

Pat the stretched dough into shape and then, using scissors or your fingertips, tear or cut away the thick edges and discard.

Spread the bread crumb mixture generously over the dough, leaving a 2-inch border. Scatter the remaining ¼ cup sugar over the bread crumbs. Transfer the apple filling to the dough, using your hands and leaving any liquid behind in the bowl. Shape the filling into a log about 2 inches from a shorter edge.

Begin rolling by lifting and pulling the bare 2-inch edge of the dough over the apple log. Tuck in the sides and, using the strudel cloth, lift and roll the strudel into a tight log with the thin layers of strudel dough encasing the filling (see page 141). The goal is to make this log firm and tight, not loose and sloppy.

Use the cloth to transfer the strudel to the prepared baking sheet, seam side down.

Brush the top and sides of the strudel with the remaining melted butter. Bake for 20 to 25 minutes, until golden brown. Cool in the pan for 10 minutes, shower with powdered sugar, and slice and serve.

If serving later, reheat for a few minutes in a 350°F oven.

PUFF PASTRY
AIRY, BUTTERY LAYERS

Mille feuille means one thousand leaves or layers: This is how the French describe puff pastry, the lovely laminated, layered, crackly dough used to make palmiers, cheese straws, and vol-au-vents. It's a lovely plank upon which to feature almost any filling, from savory roasted vegetables to sweet berries tossed in sugar. A quick puff pastry, often called rough puff, is puff pastry made (just a little bit) easier.

Make the Quick Puff Pastry, page 265, or defrost store-bought puff pastry in the refrigerator, not on the counter. Working with cold puff pastry is essential. If the butter starts to melt, it will make the dough gummy and difficult. Never hesitate to return the dough to the refrigerator to rechill it, even in the midst of decorating or working with a recipe. Keep it cold!

SHAPING AND CHILLING

Admittedly, refrigerator-cold puff pastry is challenging to roll out. You'll need some muscles. If it warms too much, the butter will smear and the layers will be compromised. So, you'll need some speed, too. Other than this challenge, puff is easy-peasy. Warm up, do some stretches, and get that puff pastry on a lightly floured surface to roll it out. If you have a stone countertop or rolling board, it helps to chill the surface with a bag of ice (then dry it well).

When it's time to fill the pastry, make sure the filling is cold, too. If it is the slightest bit warm, the butter in the dough will melt and the layers will flop. Once the pastry has been filled, chill again for at least 30 minutes before baking. This will ensure the most lift, the most layers, and the happiest baker.

Puff pastry tastes best and has the most crackly layers on the day you bake it. It can hold for one additional day—I wouldn't say no to leftover Antipasto Stromboli (page 157)—but it, and all the puff pastry recipes that follow, are better enjoyed the day they are made.

ANTIPASTO STROMBOLI

Serves 8 to 10

---

1 recipe (20 ounces, 500 g) Quick Puff Pastry, page 265, or store-bought

---

3 tablespoons tomato paste

3 anchovies, finely chopped

½ teaspoon grated garlic

8 ounces (225 g) mix of thinly sliced, Italian-style cured meats such as salami, mortadella, soppressata, and/ or capicola

4 ounces (113 g) sliced provolone cheese

½ cup (70 g) sliced roasted red pepper (about 1 pepper)

½ cup (100 g) chopped, squeeze-dried canned artichoke hearts in water (about 3)

½ cup (70 g) sliced large green pimento-stuffed olives (about 8)

3 ounces (85 g) fresh mozzarella, cut into cubes

3 pickled hot peppers, sliced

1½ teaspoons dried oregano

½ teaspoon freshly ground black pepper

1 teaspoon balsamic or red wine vinegar

2 teaspoons olive oil

Egg wash (1 egg beaten with 1 tablespoon cool water and ¼ teaspoon kosher salt)

1 tablespoon grated Parmigiano Reggiano

Stromboli, kissing cousin to the calzone, is an Italian wrap, a delicious pastry filled with goodies. Most often, stromboli is made with a yeast-raised dough, more like pizza dough, but I like the way puff pastry cooks up flaky, rich, and beautiful. A meaty, cheesy stromboli is the most sensible thing to do with the leftovers from an antipasto platter, but I like it so much, I don't wait for leftovers: I start with stromboli. Serve this at your next game day party, on the sidelines after soccer, or on the buffet table at brunch. It's savory, flavorful, and very pretty. Stromboli is a construction project, so take your time and keep chilling the pastry at every stage.

Line a baking sheet with parchment paper.

Lightly dust the counter, the puff pastry, and the rolling pin with flour. Roll out the dough to approximately 10 by 16 inches. Use a bench scraper or offset spatula to help lift and briskly transfer the dough to the parchment-lined baking sheet. Refrigerate the dough until ready to fill.

With a fork or the back of a spoon, mash the tomato paste, anchovies, and garlic into a smooth paste. Spread the paste thickly down the center of the pastry, marking off a space about 6 by 14 inches. Layer half the cured meat, half the provolone, the remaining cured meat, and the last of the provolone slices on top of the anchovy spread. Scatter the red peppers, artichoke hearts, olives, mozzarella, and pickled peppers down the center of the filling. Sprinkle with the oregano and grind black pepper over the meats and vegetables. Drizzle the filling with the vinegar and olive oil. Beautiful, right? If the pastry has warmed during this time, pop the baking sheet in the refrigerator for 20 minutes or so. It's impossible to work with puff pastry when it warms up.

(Continued)

With the 10-inch sides at the top and bottom, use a paring knife or a pizza wheel to make four diagonal slashes 1 inch apart along each long 16-inch side, from the filling to the edge. Each strip will be about 3 inches long and 1 inch wide. Fold the pastry at the top up and over the filling and do the same with the pastry at the bottom. Now, lift the left and then the right side, carrying the pastry strips up and over the filling. Starting at the top, start latticing the cut strips, slightly overlapping a bit each time. Continue like this to create a latticed effect, tucking in the last two strips. Try not to stretch the strips. Trim away any excess dough with scissors.

Get to work on the corners. There is likely to be a big lump of dough at each corner that needs to go. Gather the dough at each corner and use scissors to snip the excess. Pinch the seams together. Think rustic.

After all this handling, let the stromboli settle onto the baking sheet into a nice, plump shape, about 5 inches wide and about 13 inches long. Chill for at least 30 minutes or no more than 2 hours.

Heat the oven to 425°F and place a Baking Steel, baking stone, or inverted baking sheet on the center rack to heat as the oven heats.

Brush the surface of the stromboli with egg wash and sprinkle on the Parmesan. Bake for 55 to 60 minutes, until deeply browned. Watch, especially in the last 10 minutes, that the cheesy topping doesn't burn; if it is getting too dark, tent it with foil.

Cool slightly before slicing. May be served warm or at room temperature.

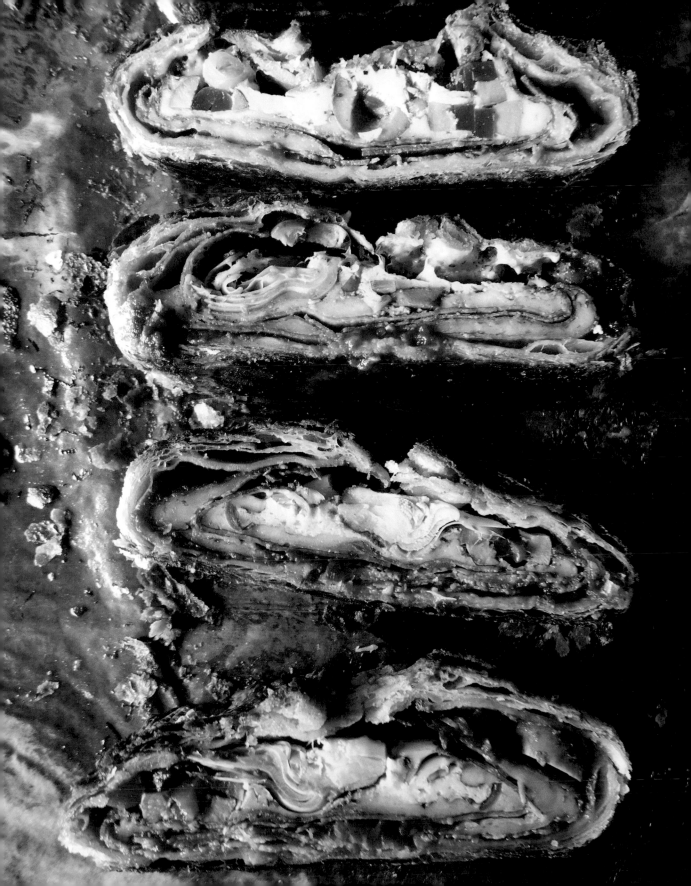

FIGGY CHEESY SPIRALS

Makes 72 appetizers

1 recipe (20 ounces, 500 g) Quick Puff Pastry, page 265, or store-bought

4 ounces (113 g) fig jam, warmed

½ teaspoon fresh thyme leaves, minced

4 ounces (113 g) Manchego, Emmenthaler, or Comté cheese, shredded

Egg wash (1 egg beaten with 1 tablespoon cool water and ¼ teaspoon kosher salt)

Spirals of puff pastry filled with jam and cheese are wonderful at the *apéro* hour, but equally delightful as "croutons" on a bright salad. The palmier, of which this is just one version, is a common pastry in France and a simple way to use puff pastry to astonish your guests. With puff in the freezer, you can make any gathering an occasion. Once you have the technique down, try sprinkling with cinnamon sugar for a sweet snack, or swab the pastry with a whisper of crème fraîche and a light brushing of sour cherry jam, or simply scatter on a generous flurry of grated cheese. This is a treat that requires no more than a little imagination and a hunt through the refrigerator. It looks, and tastes, incredibly elegant.

The jam will caramelize and darken—that's to be expected and it's delicious. Outright burned is a whole other thing. To avoid scorching, bake on two stacked baking sheets to temper the bottom heat and avoid burning the jam. Unlike many of the recipes in this book, do not use a baking stone, Baking Steel, or inverted baking sheet to cook these from the bottom.

Line a baking sheet with parchment. Lightly dust the counter, the puff pastry, and the rolling pin with flour. Divide the pastry into two equal pieces and put one back in the refrigerator. Roll out the remaining dough block to a 12-inch square and cut the pastry into two pieces, each 12 by 6 inches. Clean, sharp edges are helpful here.

Spread one-fourth of the jam very thinly from edge to edge across the surface of one sheet of the pastry, leaving a ½-inch border on one 12-inch side. You should be able to see the pastry through the jam. (If it is too thick, it will spread and burn in the oven.) Sprinkle one-fourth of the thyme over the jam. Scatter one-fourth of the cheese evenly across the surface of the jam, keeping the edge clear. Press the cheese into the jam.

Starting at the jammy 12-inch side, roll the pastry toward the bare edge, into an even, tight log that is 12 inches long and 2 inches in diameter. Keep the pastry snug.

Repeat the process with the second sheet of dough. Place the two logs on the baking sheet, cover with plastic wrap to keep the dough from drying out, and refrigerate.

Repeat the rolling out, filling, and rolling up with the remaining dough block and jam, thyme, and cheese, forming two additional logs. Place these logs on the same baking sheet, wrap well, and refrigerate for at least 30 minutes or as long as 4 hours, but no longer.

Place a rack in the center of the oven and heat to 375°F. Stack two baking sheets and put parchment on the top one. Remove two dough logs from the refrigerator. Using a very sharp knife or dental floss, cut 18 spirals from one roll by making swift slices through the roll about ¾ inch apart. Repeat with the second roll. Fiddling to make them round again, place the spirals about 1 inch apart on the prepared baking sheet; the 36 spirals will fit on one baking sheet.

Slide the stacked baking sheets onto the center rack and bake for 20 to 22 minutes, until the spirals are golden brown and bubbling. Slide the parchment with the spirals onto a cooling rack.

Reline the baking sheet with fresh parchment and repeat the cutting into spirals and baking with the 2 remaining dough logs to make 36 more spirals.

Let the pastries cool and firm up for a few minutes before serving warm or at room temperature.

The spirals may be reheated for about 6 to 8 minutes in a 350°F oven.

FRESH APRICOT BREAKFAST PASTRIES

Makes 12

1 recipe (20 ounces, 500 g) Quick Puff Pastry, page 265, or store-bought

6 ripe apricots, halved and pitted; or 3 small white peaches, pitted and quartered

1 tablespoon granulated sugar

1 tablespoon freshly squeezed lemon juice

Egg wash (1 egg beaten with 1 tablespoon cool water and ¼ teaspoon kosher salt)

Pastry Cream, page 129, cold

3 tablespoons apricot jam, heated and strained

Powdered sugar, for dusting

I am weak as a kitten around ripe apricots; I'll eat them until my stomach hurts. I had my first ever as a 24-year-old traveling in Italy and forevermore looked for that tart, sweet, glorious sunny flavor. This elegant pastry is usually found in the most swish of Parisian patisseries, yet it's dead simple to make once you've mastered quick puff and pastry cream, two skills that are always good to have in your arsenal. Cut the fruit at the very last minute and toss with the lemon juice right away so it will not oxidize and discolor. Pay close attention to the quality of the fruit and make sure they are the same size with no bruises—and these pastries will look very fancy indeed. Apricot is the classic flavor, but apricots can be difficult to find on the East Coast, so I often substitute white peaches, which hold a similar, though more floral, allure. You could also substitute blueberries, raspberries, halved pitted cherries or plums, or any combination of summer fruit.

Line a baking sheet with parchment. Lightly dust the counter, the puff pastry, and the rolling pin with flour. Roll out the dough to a 16- by 12-inch rectangle and cut into 12 (4-inch) squares.

Stir the fruit, sugar, and lemon juice together. Place the pastry squares on the parchment-lined baking sheet spaced evenly apart. Using a paring knife, make a shallow knife slash around each square, ½ inch from the edges. Dock the center of each square by making a shallow X, again, not slicing all the way through.

Paint the egg wash on the edges of each square. Pipe or spoon about 2 tablespoons pastry cream in the center. Chill the pastries for 30 minutes before baking.

(Continued)

Heat the oven to 400°F.

Top the pastry cream with the apricot halves, rounded side up. Slide the pastries into the oven and bake for 20 to 25 minutes. The pastry will turn deeply golden brown and the fruit and pastry cream will get very gently freckled here and there. Remove from the oven and brush the surface of the fruit with the warm jam.

Cool a little before serving, then dust generously with powdered sugar and dig in. If you choose to stand over the pastries as they cool to smell the warm apricots mingling with the vanilla-scented pastry cream, who am I to stop you?

PHYLLO
SHATTERING, CRISPY LAYERS

Phyllo dough is made up of wispy sheets of nothing more than flour and water. I bathe the airy sheets in butter, to make up for none in the dough, and layer them to form a shell of crackly, bronzed, parchment-like leaves that surround a rich filling. I've never tried to make my own phyllo, especially after an article in the *New York Times* by Yotam Ottolenghi convinced me it would be absolute madness. For years, I have relied on the easy-to-find frozen packages of phyllo, but my friend Mary Reilly ruined me forever when she introduced me to the Poseidon Bakery in New York City (9th Avenue between 44th and 45th), where the phyllo is handmade and truly glorious. Now, I feel I must urge you to do some Googling. See if any bakery or restaurant in your town makes phyllo and be prepared to *oooh* and *aaaah*. It's not about flavor—there are too few ingredients for that to be the case. It's about the feel, the velvety softness, and how easy it is to work with. Be assured, the store-bought version will work perfectly well with all of these recipes—but oh, the joy of handmade phyllo!

The phyllo sheets found in the supermarket freezer section come in many sizes. During testing for this book, we found packages that held sheets 9 by 14 inches and 14 by 16 inches, and the handmade sheets were a generous 16 by 18 inches. Because of this variety, your yield may vary. Use your best judgement when it comes to cutting the strips of buttered, layered sheets. I like a small bite, just 3 inches wide, but if the phyllo is 14 inches, it divides into 3½-inch-wide strips more easily. To get past all the inconsistencies (which I try my best to avoid in a cookbook), the following phyllo recipes use 14- by 16-inch sheets.

PHYLLO STRATEGIES

Defrost the phyllo overnight in the refrigerator. Do not try to speed things up with the microwave or by leaving it on the counter to defrost. There is simply no way to defrost phyllo quickly.

To set up a phyllo workspace, place a generous piece of plastic wrap on the counter. It should be larger than the sheets of phyllo when unrolled, with the long edge parallel to the edge of the counter. Building a buttery phyllo pastry on top of plastic makes it so much easier to lift the pastry from the counter. Unroll the phyllo sheets next to this workspace and place another piece of plastic wrap over them. Finally, cover the stack of phyllo with a damp kitchen towel.

Work with one sheet at a time on the plastic-covered portion of the counter. Have clarified butter (see box) close at hand. I opt for a silicone brush for phyllo as it's less apt to catch on the sheets. Know that it's common for the sheet to split or tear a little. Put the parts together on the plastic wrap and use the butter to glue it back together. Dab with the brush rather than sweeping it across the dough. Be generous with the butter, then place another sheet over the first and repeat, using the butter to glue the sheets and any tears or rips together. Finally, top with a third buttered sheet.

Use a pizza wheel or a chef's knife to cleanly slice the stacked sheets into long 3-inch-wide strips to either roll up like a cigar (Cranberry–Goat Cheese Faux Strudelettes, page 173) or fold like a flag to make triangles (Tyropita, page 171). Fillings should be enthusiastically spiced and refrigerator cold, with a sturdy, not-at-all-wet texture so the phyllo sheets don't get mushy. Chill or freeze the pastries if you will not be baking them immediately.

PHYLLO IS FREEZER FRIENDLY

It's worth taking some time to make dozens of phyllo triangles or cigars at once. Invite a friend and prepare for the party season. Freeze the butter-coated, unbaked pastries on a baking sheet lined with parchment until frozen hard, about 1 hour. Then transfer to a ziptop bag or freezer container. Bake the pastries straight from the freezer (after another butter bath) for a few minutes more than the time listed in the recipe, using visual cues like browning, bubbling, and crisping to determine the right amount of time.

PHYLLO'S BETTER BUTTER

Clarifying is a technique that separates the butter from milk solids that might scorch in the oven. To clarify butter, melt it over medium-high heat until foamy. Pour the melted butter into a glass measuring cup (or another heatproof glass container). Let the butter sit for a few minutes while the milk solids drop to the bottom of the cup. Pour the clear yellow butter into a small bowl and use that, without the milk solids, to brush on phyllo. Clarified butter does not burn as readily and achieves a lovely, even burnish. For brushing phyllo, I use salted butter. It adds to the flavor of store-bought phyllo, particularly. If your household never ever has salted butter, add ⅛ teaspoon kosher salt to each 8 tablespoons (113 g) butter as it is melting.

TYROPITA (CHEESE-FILLED TRIANGLES)

Makes 24

8 ounces (225 g)
phyllo sheets

1 cup (113 g)
crumbled feta
cheese

½ cup (113 g)
ricotta cheese

½ cup (50 g)
grated Parmigiano
Reggiano

½ cup (50 g)
grated Pecorino

1 egg, lightly
beaten

½ cup (50 g) finely
chopped scallions,
white and green
parts (about 4)

¼ cup (15 g)
chopped fresh
flat-leaf parsley

2 teaspoons
dried mint, or
2 tablespoons
finely chopped
fresh mint

½ teaspoon
freshly ground
black pepper

8 tablespoons
(113 g) salted
butter, clarified
(see box, page
169)

These adorable cheese-filled flaky pastries are surprisingly easy to make. They're delicious either warm or at room temperature, and have a satisfying crackle. The cheese is sharp, slightly funky, and speckled with green from scallions and herbs. Be generous with the buttering of the phyllo sheets. I'm a fan of dried mint and opt for it here, but if you have fresh mint at hand, there's no harm in substituting it.

Defrost the phyllo overnight in the refrigerator.

Stir together the feta, ricotta, Parmigiano Reggiano, Pecorino, egg, scallion, parsley, mint, and pepper. Chill the filling while preparing the phyllo sheets.

Line two baking sheets with parchment paper. Heat the oven to 400°F and place the racks above and below the center mark.

Set up an area on the counter to work and line it with a piece of plastic wrap. Unfurl the phyllo sheets and cover with a sheet of plastic wrap and then a clean damp kitchen towel (see page 168).

Peel off a sheet of phyllo and place it on the plastic wrap. Brush this phyllo sheet generously with butter. Stack the next sheet on top of the last and brush with butter again. Repeat one more time, until there are three sheets stacked and buttered. Slice the stacked sheets into six sections, each about 2½ inches wide and 14 inches long.

Place a scant 1 tablespoon filling ½ inch from the end of one strip of phyllo. Grasping the right lower corner of the phyllo strip, fold the phyllo across the filling, forming a tiny cheese-filled triangle (see photo, page 166). Continue to fold the triangle over itself, as though folding a flag. It doesn't need to be tight or snug. Let the butter be the glue that holds it all together. Place the cheese triangle seam-side down on one prepared baking sheet and generously butter the top and sides. Continue with the remaining phyllo sheets until there are six adorable little cheese triangles.

Repeat three times with the remaining phyllo sheets, three at a time, making six cheese pies with each 3-sheet stack for a total of 24 triangles on the two baking sheets.

Give them all another butter bath and slide the baking sheets into the oven. Bake for 10 minutes. Rotate and swap the position of the baking sheets and bake for another 10 to 15 minutes, until the pastries are golden brown and flaky.

Cool several minutes before serving.

CRANBERRY-GOAT CHEESE FAUX STRUDELETTES

Makes 24

8 ounces (225 g) phyllo sheets

———

¼ cup (50 g) granulated sugar

⅓ cup (80 ml) water

2 tablespoons freshly squeezed orange juice

½ teaspoon ground cinnamon

1 cup (100 g) fresh or frozen whole cranberries

½ cup (57 g) pecans, toasted and chopped

3 tablespoons dried cranberries

3 tablespoons finely chopped crystallized ginger

3 ounces (85 g) soft goat cheese

———

8 tablespoons (113 g) salted butter, clarified (see box, page 169)

This recipe is for those of you who yearn to stretch strudel but haven't quite taken the leap. (Do it. It's easier than you think. See page 138.) Here phyllo stands in for strudel's layers, buttery and as thin as parchment. The filling takes advantage of cranberries' ability to shift from sweet to savory. I love cranberries' ruby red bursts of tart in every incarnation: They take on sweet easily, have an affinity for soft, creamy cheeses, and are ready to sidle up to toasted nuts like old friends. It was with all that in mind, riffing off a well-loved family recipe for chutney, that I created these strudelettes. The filling expands when it heats, so keep the rolls a little loose. Serve as an appetizer, with a cheese course, or as dessert with goat's milk or crème fraîche ice cream. There will be some left-over filling; serve it as a spread with crackers.

Defrost the phyllo overnight in the refrigerator.

Bring the sugar, water, orange juice, and cinnamon to boil in a medium saucepan over high heat. Add the cranberries, stir, and reduce the heat to medium. Let the cranberries cook in the sugar syrup until they burst and the sauce has thickened, 16 to 18 minutes. Stir in the pecans, dried cranberries, and ginger pieces. The cranberry conserve will last up to a month in the refrigerator. Cool completely before filling the phyllo.

Pinch off pieces of the goat cheese and stir into the cranberry mixture. It should be chunky with nubbins of cheese.

Line two baking sheets with parchment paper. Heat the oven to 400°F and place the racks above and below the center mark.

(Continued)

Set up an area on the counter to work and line it with a piece of plastic wrap. Unfurl the phyllo sheets and cover with a sheet of plastic wrap and then a clean damp kitchen towel (see page 168).

Peel off a sheet of phyllo and place it on the plastic wrap. Brush this phyllo sheet generously with butter. Stack the next sheet on top of the last and brush generously with butter. Repeat until three sheets are stacked and buttered. Slice the stacked sheets into six sections, each about 2½ inches wide.

Place a generous 1 tablespoon of filling ½ inch from the short edge of each section of phyllo. Roll up the filling in the buttered sheets, gently tucking in the sides so that it is shaped like a cigar. Place seam-side down on one baking sheet and generously butter the outside, especially on the sides (if overlooked, they will not brown as well as the top). Continue with the remaining phyllo sheets until there are six adorable little cranberry logs.

Repeat three more times with the remaining phyllo sheets, three at a time, making six strudelettes with each three-sheet stack for a total of 24 strudelettes on the two baking sheets.

Give them all another butter bath, slide the baking sheets into the oven, and bake for 10 minutes. Rotate and swap the position of the baking sheets and bake for 15 minutes longer, until the strudelettes are golden brown and flaky.

Cool several minutes before serving. I like to serve one or two per person, sliced in half diagonally to expose the filling. They are delicious at room temperature, too.

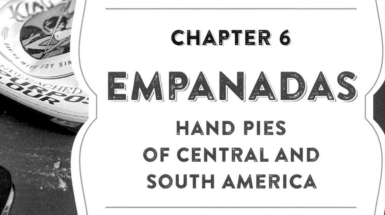

CHAPTER 6
EMPANADAS
HAND PIES OF CENTRAL AND SOUTH AMERICA

Whether baked or fried, empanadas, the hand pies of Central and South America, are fashioned into half-moons, rounds, triangles, or pyramids made to stand on end. Whatever their shape, they satisfy the hungries.

Here, I'm offering recipes for empanadas shaped like half-moons with a simple crimp, or a turned, rolled edge called a *repulgue*. It's the perfect shape for the snack-sized empanada, but when it came to the smaller appetizer version, *empanaditas,* pages 190 to 193, I played with some fanciful shapes, just for fun. If you're not feeling fancy, a classic half-moon will work for every recipe.

BAKED OR FRIED

While there are more than a dozen versions of empanada dough that show up on a Google search, for my purposes, the Cream Cheese Pie Dough (page 252) works beautifully for baked empanadas. It is sturdy, yet tender, and I use it to wrap up any filling for baked empanadas. Shortening Pie Dough (page 253) fits the bill, too, with a sandy texture and a longer lasting flake.

A fried empanada requires a different dough entirely. Empanada Dough That's Fit to Be Fried (page 268) has the qualities necessary to hold together under high temperatures and to cook thoroughly in a short period of time. It is a dough that is elastic enough to stretch around the fillings, and sturdy enough to hold a firmly crimped edge in the hot oil. Made with shortening or lard, it will rise up, blistering and crackling, in the high heat of the oil.

FORMING AND CRIMPING EMPANADAS

For baked empanadas, make two batches of the Cream Cheese Pie Dough (page 252), working with one and keeping the other chilled and covered with plastic wrap. Mark a 15-inch square on the work surface using painter's or masking tape. Lightly flour the counter. Roll the dough to 5 by 15 inches, about ⅛ inch thick. Use a cookie cutter, plate, bowl, or (traditionally) an old-fashioned coffee can to cut out three 5-inch disks. Discard the scraps.

The filling should be cold. I like to use a 3-tablespoon scoop to portion out the filling for each dough round. Hold one dough disk flat in your palm (if you prefer to work on the counter, make sure there is enough flour to keep the dough moving freely) and paint the edge with your fingertip or a pastry brush dipped in cold water. Place the filling in the center of the disk and pull the sides up, stretching the dough over the filling to form a half-moon. (Photos 1 and 2.) Firmly pinch the edge together to seal.

Fold in the corner, then work your way around the edges, folding in a small bit along the edge of the dough to cover up any ragged edges. All empanadas should start with this tidy action before crimping to decorate and seal. There are two ways to seal, or crimp, the empanada: Press the tines of a table fork along the edge for a classic **fork crimp.** Or, to make a *repulgue,* **or rolled edge,** turn in the corner of the sealed edge and then lift and turn segments of the edge all the way around. (Photos 3 and 4.) A roll will form, and the roll will become more beautiful and more consistent with each subsequent empanada. Your first few attempts will be a little rough, but just keep working to make an even, plump, and round *repulgue*.

Little empanadas, *empanaditas*, are marvelous snacks or passed appetizers. Roll the dough to 6 by 12 inches and cut out eight 2½-inch rounds. Lifting one at a time, paint the edge with cold water, and top with a skimpy tablespoon of filling, then fold and finish as with a larger empanada, using any of the classic crimps.

But this is also the perfect opportunity to work some magic, forming *empanadita*-sized stars, flowers, or caps (see page 191 for a photograph of these shapes).

To make a **star,** hold a round dough disk in your palm and paint the edge with cold water. Pinch the edge of the round together firmly, making one of the five points. Place a skimpy tablespoon of filling next to the pleat. Now work around the circle, pinching four additional points. Pinch with vigor, not shyly, or the little star will open flat in the oven and look more like a moon. Chill the *empanaditas* for a few minutes before baking, to help hold their shape.

To make a **cap,** paint the edge of a 3-inch round with cold water. Place about 1½ tablespoons filling (more than for the other *empanaditas,* because there is twice the amount of dough). Stack a second dough disk on top of the first and press the edge firmly together. Finish this cap with a *repulgue.*

To make a **flower,** cut out 3-inch squares and paint the edges of one with cold water. Place a skimpy tablespoon of filling in the center of the square and lift the four corners up, toward the center. Pinch the tips together firmly and release; the pastry will settle into a square shape with four eyelets forming a flower shape through which the filling will shine.

SERVING AND STORING

Empanadas are delicious all by themselves, hot from the oven or at room temperature, but they also benefit from a lip-smacking sauce. I've included chimichurri here, but I embrace queso, guacamole, an herb- and garlic-laced mayonnaise as appropriate dunking sauces. Expert empanada eaters nip off the triangular tip and spoon sauce right on top of the exposed filling.

To freeze empanadas before baking: Place the unbaked empanadas on a parchment lined baking sheet and freeze hard, about an hour. Store in a ziptop bag and freeze for up to 3 months. Bake the empanadas while still frozen for 5 to 8 minutes longer than the time stated in the recipe, or until the crust is golden brown and the filling is steaming hot.

TURKEY PICADILLO EMPANADAS

Makes 18

2 tablespoons grapeseed or canola oil

1 cup (142 g) diced white onion (about 1 medium)

2 garlic cloves, finely chopped

1 pound (450 g) ground turkey, dark and light meat or all dark meat

1 cup (225 g) canned crushed tomatoes

¼ cup (35 g) sliced small green pimento-stuffed olives, plus 2 tablespoons of their brine

¼ cup (45 g) golden raisins, soaked in hot water for 1 hour, then drained

2 eggs, hard-boiled and chopped

1 tablespoon Worcestershire sauce

½ teaspoon dried marjoram or Mexican oregano

½ teaspoon cumin seeds

½ teaspoon kosher salt

½ teaspoon freshly ground black pepper

———

2 recipes Cream Cheese Pie Dough (page 252), formed into 3- by 4-inch rectangular blocks

———

Egg wash (1 egg beaten with 1 tablespoon cool water and ¼ teaspoon kosher salt)

A picadillo is a stew particular to many Central and South American countries, Cuba, and elsewhere. It's a snazzy, textural mix-up of sweet and savory, often containing olives, pickles, dried fruit and/or nuts, and I'm crazy about it. If you aren't an olive person, omit them, and the same goes for the raisins, but in my turkey version I've added them all. Serve with guacamole, sour cream, queso, and hot sauce.

In a 10-inch, heavy skillet, warm the oil over medium-high heat until shimmering. Add the onion and cook until wilted and starting to brown at the edges, about 5 minutes. Stir in the garlic and cook for an additional minute before adding the turkey. Using two wooden spoons, break up the turkey meat and cook until the pink is gone. Stir in the crushed tomatoes and bring to a boil, then reduce the temperature and simmer until slightly thickened, about 15 minutes.

Stir in the olives and their brine, the raisins, eggs, Worcestershire, marjoram, cumin seeds, salt, and pepper. Set aside to cool completely.

Heat the oven to 400°F and place two racks above and below the center point. Line two baking sheets with parchment paper.

On a lightly floured counter, roll out one dough block to a 15-inch square and cut out 9 (5-inch) rounds. With a fingertip dipped in cool water, dampen the edge of one dough round and place in your palm. Add a scant ¼ cup filling and fold the dough in half, stretching it over the filling. Pinch the empanada edge together, then decoratively pleat or crimp (see page 178). Place on one baking sheet and repeat with the remaining rounds of dough.

Repeat with the second block of dough, filling the second baking sheet. Paint the empanadas with the egg wash.

Bake on the two racks for 25 minutes, until golden brown. Halfway through baking, switch the baking sheets top to bottom and front to back. Cool slightly and serve.

PORK PASTOR EMPANADAS

Makes 18

1 tablespoon grapeseed or canola oil

1 cup (142 g) diced white onion (about 1 medium)

3 garlic cloves, minced

1 pound (450 g) ground pork

1 or 2 chipotles from canned chipotle in adobo, plus 3 tablespoons of their adobo sauce (optional, spicy)

2 tablespoons fresh lime juice

2 tablespoons apple cider vinegar

1 teaspoon marjoram or Mexican oregano

1½ teaspoons kosher salt

¾ teaspoon freshly ground black pepper

1 cup (255 g) drained crushed pineapple

¼ cup (15 g) roughly chopped cilantro leaves and stems

2 recipes Cream Cheese Pie Dough (page 252), formed into 3- by 4-inch rectangular blocks

Egg wash (1 egg beaten with 1 tablespoon cool water and ¼ teaspoon kosher salt)

Chimichurri (recipe follows), optional

Tacos *al pastor* offers up an irresistible combination of succulent pork, acidic sweet pineapple, and chile heat that makes me happy. In this empanada, the filling reflects those glorious flavors, but without the hours of slow cooking. Chipotles in adobo add significant heat to your filling, so proceed with caution. I will happily add as much as two entire chipotles (diced) to the mix, but that makes it hot as . . . well let's just say, it's pretty piquant. Use fresh or canned pineapple, draining it well before adding it to the pork mixture; a wet filling makes a soggy empanada.

In a large wide skillet, warm the oil over medium-high heat until shimmering. Add the onion and cook until wilted and starting to brown at the edges, about 8 minutes. Stir in the garlic and cook for an additional minute, then add the pork. Using two wooden spoons, break up the meat and cook until the pink is gone. Stir in the chipotle and adobo sauce (if using), the lime juice, vinegar, marjoram, salt, and pepper. Cook until most of the liquid has evaporated, about 2 minutes. Stir in the pineapple and cilantro, remove from the heat, and set aside to cool.

Heat the oven to 400°F and place two racks above and below the center point of the oven. Line two baking sheets with parchment paper.

On a lightly floured counter, roll out one dough block to a 15-inch square and cut out 9 (5-inch) rounds. With a fingertip dipped in cool water, dampen the edge of one dough round and place in your palm. Add a scant ¼ cup filling and fold the dough in half, stretching it over the filling. Pinch the empanada edge together, then decoratively pleat or crimp (see page 178). Place on one baking sheet and repeat with the remaining rounds of dough. Repeat with the second block of dough, filling the second baking sheet. Paint the empanadas with the egg wash.

Bake on the two racks for 25 minutes, until golden brown. Halfway through baking, switch the baking sheets top to bottom and front to back. Cool slightly and serve with chimichurri.

CHIMICHURRI

Makes 1 ½ cups

3 tablespoons apple cider vinegar

¼ cup (25 g) minced shallots

2 teaspoons minced garlic

½ to 1 teaspoon minced small Thai bird or other very spicy red chile

1 teaspoon kosher salt

½ cup (30 g) finely chopped fresh flat-leaf parsley leaves

½ cup (30 g) finely chopped cilantro leaves and stems

½ cup (30 g) finely chopped fresh basil leaves

1 tablespoon finely chopped fresh mint leaves

¾ cup (180 ml) olive oil

Meaty or cheesy empanadas are delicious all on their own, but chimichurri adds a green, herbal freshness that can't be beat. I use this sauce with abandon on so many dishes: Grilled fish! Roasted potatoes! Steamed vegetables! I like the snap of the hot chiles, but you should omit them if you're not a fan. For more salty umami, make it a salsa verde by adding 2 chopped anchovies and 2 tablespoons rinsed capers.

Combine the vinegar, shallot, garlic, chile, and salt in a small bowl and let it sit for about 10 minutes to slightly pickle. Stir in the parsley, cilantro, basil, and mint. Use a small whisk or a fork to add the olive oil slowly, to fully combine with the vinegar so it will not separate as it sits. It should be a thick saucy mixture. Cover and chill for 2 hours or up to overnight before bringing to room temperature and serving alongside hot empanadas.

OOZY CHEESE FRIED EMPANADAS

Makes 9

1 batch Empanada Dough That's Fit to Be Fried (page 268)

14 ounces (400 g) Oaxacan or Monterey Jack cheese, shredded (4 cups)

½ cup or more Pickled Red Onion (recipe follows), drained (optional)

About 1 quart vegetable oil, for frying

Fried empanadas filled with melty cheese barely make it to the table; they are so appealing everyone gathers around the pan, risking it all for that hopping-hot filling. Traditionalists serve the crunchy wonders with a sugar coating once out of the fryer, but I like the briny counterpoint of pickled onions stuffed inside instead. (To make the sweet version, omit the onions and thickly dust the empanadas with powdered sugar when they emerge from the fryer.) Measure small plates and bowls to find a 5-inch round. Coffee cans are often the right size.

Line a baking sheet with parchment paper. On a lightly floured counter, roll out the dough to a 15-inch square and cut out 9 (5-inch) rounds. With a fingertip dipped in cool water, dampen the edge of one dough round and place in your palm. Add a generous 3 tablespoons shredded cheese and 3 or 4 strands of onion pickle. Fold the dough in half, stretching it over the filling, and pinch the empanada edge together, then fold the edge in and fork-crimp (see page 178). Place on the baking sheet and repeat with the remaining rounds of dough. Refrigerate while the oil comes to temperature.

Set up a baking sheet with a rack over it, then line the sheet with paper towels. Heat 2 inches oil in a wide straight-sided skillet over medium-high heat; use a thermometer to gauge the temperature: When the oil reaches 350°F, add about 3 empanadas and cook, turning once, for about 6 minutes total, until browned, crisp, and blistered. Place on the paper towels as they are removed from the oil. Repeat with the remaining empanadas and serve immediately.

PICKLED RED ONION

Makes 2 cups

1 large red onion, sliced in ⅛-inch-thick half-moons (about 2 cups, 285 g)

½ cup (120 ml) apple cider vinegar

½ cup (120 ml) water

1 teaspoon pickling spice

½ teaspoon kosher salt

1 (2-inch) swath peeled lemon zest

Quick to make and easy to add to just about anything, this is my go-to pickle. There will be more than needed for the cheese empanadas, but you will not have any regrets. They're fantastic on a sandwich, next to grilled or roasted meat or poultry, or straight from the jar.

Place the onion slices in a glass jar with a lid. In a small saucepan, combine the vinegar, water, pickling spice, salt, and lemon peel. Bring to a boil, then pour over the onions. Let them sit for 20 minutes and they're ready to eat. Or cool thoroughly, cover, and refrigerate. The onions will be delicious for a week or more.

CHAI-SPICED PLUM AND WALNUT EMPANADITAS

Makes 25

½ teaspoon loose black tea

¼ teaspoon cardamom seeds

¼ teaspoon anise or fennel seeds

¼ teaspoon freshly ground black pepper

1 pound (450 g) dark purple plums, pitted and chopped

1 cup (200 g) granulated sugar

1 teaspoon lemon juice

1 tablespoon aged balsamic vinegar

⅓ cup (30 g) walnuts, toasted and finely chopped

1 recipe Cream Cheese Pie Dough (page 252), formed into a 3- by 4-inch rectangular block

Egg wash (1 egg beaten with 1 tablespoon cool water and ¼ teaspoon kosher salt)

This highly spiced filling makes these *empanaditas* an excellent partner for cheese or chocolate. Plums require a more watchful eye during cooking because of their water content. Stir and be vigilant or the jam will scorch. To form stars, caps, or flower shapes, see page 180.

In a small saucepan over medium-high heat, toast the tea, cardamom, anise, and black pepper until fragrant, just about 2 minutes. Add the plums, sugar, and lemon juice. With the heat still at medium-high, mash the ingredients with a potato masher or the back of a sturdy spoon and cook until thick and sticky and reduced to about 1 cup, 20 to 25 minutes. Stir constantly so it does not scorch. Remove from the heat, sprinkle with the balsamic, and stir in the walnuts. Cool the filling entirely before proceeding. The filling will keep, covered and refrigerated, for 1 week.

Heat the oven to 400°F and place a rack in the center. Line a baking sheet with parchment paper. On a lightly floured counter, roll out the dough block to a 12-inch square and cut out 25 (2½-inch) rounds. With a fingertip dipped in cool water, dampen the edge of one dough round and place in your palm. Add a scant 1½ teaspoons plum filling and fold the dough in half, stretching it over the filling. Pinch the *empanadita* edge together, then decoratively pleat or crimp (see page 178). Place on the baking sheet and repeat with the remaining rounds of dough. Use a fork to make a few vent holes in the top of each half-moon and then paint the tops with the egg wash.

Bake until golden brown, about 20 minutes. Cool slightly before serving.

SWEET TOMATO JAM EMPANADITAS

Makes 25

---

2 pounds (900 g) ripe tomatoes, cut into ½-inch dice

¾ cup (150 g) packed brown sugar

¼ cup (50 g) granulated sugar

6 tablespoons (90 ml) fresh lime juice

6 tablespoons (90 ml) apple cider vinegar

½ medium jalapeño, seeded and minced

1 teaspoon grated fresh ginger

½ teaspoon ground cinnamon

1 teaspoon kosher salt

¼ teaspoon freshly ground black pepper

---

1 recipe Cream Cheese Pie Dough (page 252), formed into a 3- by 4-inch rectangular block

¼ cup (38 g) crumbled cotija or feta cheese

¼ cup (30 g) packed cilantro leaves

Egg wash (1 egg beaten with 1 tablespoon cool water and ¼ teaspoon kosher salt)

The rich, jammy tomato filling amplifies the cool of crumbly cheese topped off with a fresh bite of cilantro. Make them for pass-around appetizers or the buffet table: two-bite hand-held snacks, the entirely different, utterly delectable little *empanadita*. Make the half-moons, or practice your best star, cap, or flower shape (see page 191) for a showy addition to the potluck table. After forming 25, you will have extra tomato jam. Lucky you. It's delicious smeared inside a grilled cheese sandwich.

In a heavy, non-reactive, 3-quart saucepan, bring the tomatoes, brown and granulated sugars, lime juice, vinegar, jalapeño, ginger, cinnamon, salt, and black pepper to a boil over medium-high heat. Reduce the heat and simmer for about 1 hour, until thick and jammy, stirring frequently especially as it is closer to being done. It's ready when a spoonful has the texture of preserves, salsa, or chutney. It's heavy and dense without being watery. Cool completely before filling the empanadas. The filling will keep, covered and refrigerated, for 1 week.

Heat the oven to 400°F and place a rack in the center. Line a baking sheet with parchment paper.

On a lightly floured counter, roll out the dough block to a 12-inch square and cut out 25 (2½-inch) rounds. With a fingertip dipped in cool water, dampen the edge of one dough round and place in your palm. Add a scant tablespoon tomato jam, a nubbin of cheese, and one or two cilantro leaves. For stars, caps, or flowers, see page 180 for instructions. Or fold the dough round in half, stretching it over the filling, and pinch the *empanadita* edge together. Decoratively pleat or crimp (see page 178). Place on the baking sheet and

repeat with the remaining rounds of dough. Paint the top of the *empanaditas* with the egg wash. They do not need to be vented.

Bake until golden brown, about 20 minutes. Cool slightly before serving.

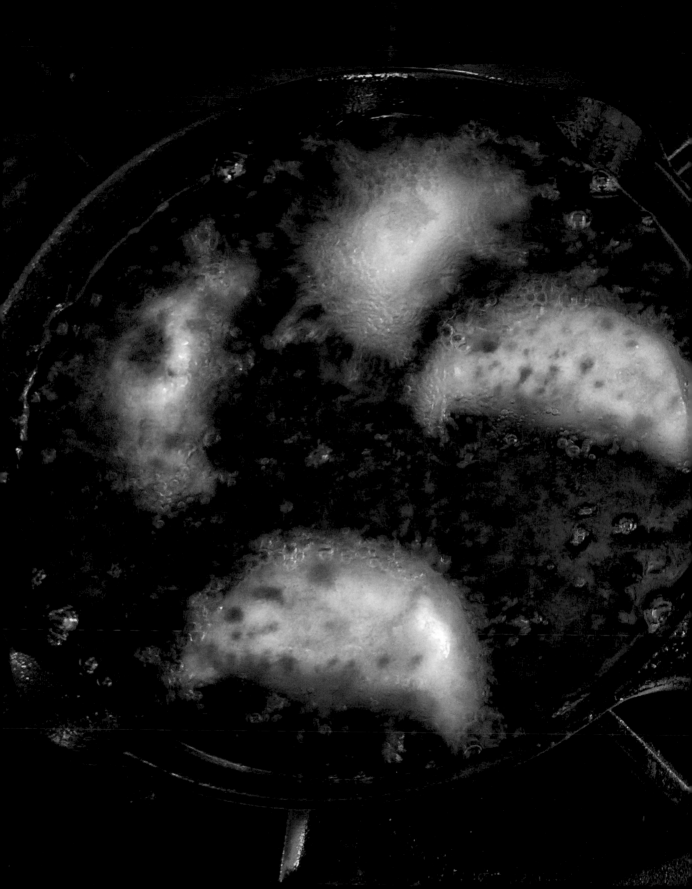

CHAPTER 7

FILLED AND FRIED

PIES MEET HOT OIL

Admit it, fried foods are delicious. No, we shouldn't be eating them every day, but can't we feel a little good about fried spring rolls stuffed full of vegetables? Or crackly dough surrounding lots of fruit? Sure we can.

There are just two of us and there are times when I make dinner and it looks like I've cooked for eight. I can't help myself. Fortunately, we both work at home, and leftovers are great for lunch. Once. But what to do with the bits that linger? Spring roll wrappers come to the rescue. Tuck just about anything in a wrapper and quickly shallow-fry for another surefire way of repurposing leftovers. And then there are times when I make fried food not to be virtuous and avoid wasting food, but simply to enjoy the pleasure of a fried fruit pie with buttermilk dough.

SUCCESSFUL FRYING

I know Fear of Frying is real. That's why I'm setting you up to shallow-fry in a skillet with only about 2 cups of oil. I love my 12-inch cast-iron skillet for this sort of kitchen work. And the oil is great for the pan—there is no better way to season your cast iron than to fry in it!

Use an instant-read thermometer to monitor the temperature of the oil. When the pies are lowered into the pan, they will lower the temperature of the oil. Compensate by increasing the heat under the pan at that point; but be very careful and continually fiddle with the heat under the pan because in an instant, the oil can get overly hot and scorch the pies. Monitor throughout with the thermometer. Working without one is possible, but it's easier to achieve consistent results using one.

When frying food, do not walk away from the stove. If you must, take the pan off the heat. Use long-handled tongs to turn the pies. Water or any moisture will cause spattering, which is scary, so make sure fillings are only very slightly moist at most. Seal the pies well and carefully, so no filling will escape.

A not-at-all scientific survey of my friends revealed that Fear of Frying is not only about the frying itself, but disposing of that pesky oil is also an issue. First of all, you're going to wait until it's cold before doing anything. Totally cold. And you're going to keep a funnel in the kitchen. The oil can be strained and reused two or three times, unless it develops a strong flavor. Smell or taste the cold oil to see if it remains neutral. With only 2 or 3 cups of oil, a manageable quantity, use a clean, quart-sized, lidded glass jar to store it for the next use. Place it in the refrigerator.

Once it's time to dispose of the oil, find a bottle or jar with a lid that is headed for recycling, and funnel that oil right into the jar, cap it, and throw it away. (Once filled with oil, jars can't be recycled, sadly.)

Fried pies are best when eaten shortly after they emerge from the frying pan. I wish there was a successful way to freeze and reheat any of these fried treats, but they just don't taste as delicious as when they are freshly made. It is possible to freeze the pies before frying, then fry directly from the freezer.

HOW TO FRY A FRUIT PIE

Many, many years ago, on a winding road trip from Pennsylvania to Florida, I traveled through South Carolina along some back roads. A gas station stop provided my first introduction to some of the greatest food this country has to offer: country ham and biscuits, pimento cheese sandwiches, and fried apple pies. I've long since learned how to make a biscuit, where to get great country ham, and how to stir together pimento cheese, but the secret to fried pies eluded me.

When I sat down to write this book, I was determined to crack the fried pie code. I cut up

fresh fruit, added sugar and cornstarch, as I might when making a regular fruit pie, and wrapped my favorite pie dough around the filling. The pie opened in the hot oil making a spattering mess. I tried with other doughs, with less filling, and with all sorts of shapes and crimping techniques, but still I had pies that did not hold together and fruit that floated in the hot oil.

Seeking an expert, I contacted Ronni Lundy, author of *Victuals: An Appalachian Journey, with Recipes,* and she straightened me right out. First of all, the classic fried pie is made with dried fruit. This, of course, made sense. The wet fillings interfered with the seal on the dough and were more likely to sneak out into the oil.

The dough still remained a mystery. Ronni's own dough uses lard at room temperature, and soon I understood the value of a dough made with emulsified fats over one studded with pebbles of cold butter. When the pies hit the hot oil, those large butter or fat pebbles melted and left a hole in the dough where the filling escaped.

With Ronni's recipe in mind and the ratios I've used for all my pie doughs, I made a buttermilk-based dough with room-temperature shortening that mixed in smoothly, leaving no pebbles to encourage seepage. The buttermilk provides tang and its acidity gives a little lift to the dough, for layers of crispy, satisfying crunch.

A fried pie is a delight. It's perfect summer food, easily cobbled together with just a handful of fresh fruit balanced with an equal amount of dried fruit. Its fresh flavor sings, the dried fruit helps with texture and absorbs extra liquid, and the whole is a delicious treat your family will adore.

VEGETARIAN SPRING ROLLS

Makes about 16

2 tablespoons grapeseed or canola oil

6 ounces (170 g) shiitake mushrooms, stems discarded and caps slivered

2 tablespoons finely grated fresh ginger

1 tablespoon finely grated garlic

¼ cup (15 g) chopped cilantro stems

3 cups (450 g) shredded napa cabbage

2 cups (100 g) shredded carrots

¼ cup (60 ml) mirin (rice wine)

2 tablespoons low-sodium soy sauce or tamari

1 tablespoon toasted sesame oil

1 cup (113 g) snap peas, each cut into two or three pieces

½ cup (50 g) chopped scallions, green and white parts (about 4)

¼ cup (15 g) chopped cilantro leaves

About 16 spring roll wrappers

2 to 3 cups (480 to 720 ml) grapeseed, peanut, or canola oil, for frying

Sweet, Salty, Spicy Dipping Sauce (recipe follows), for serving (optional)

Spring rolls are surprisingly easy and satisfying. You'll find the wrappers in the refrigerated section of the grocery store, (inexplicably) near the tofu and tortillas, or in the freezer section at an Asian grocer in affordable packs of 50 or 100. I won't pretend there isn't some knife work involved in chopping the vegetables for the filling, but I tend to cook one thing while chopping the next and it all comes together happily. Or use the food processor to shred the cabbage and carrots for a jumpstart on the chopping. Make the filling earlier in the day or even the day before, then roll 'em up for dinner. Get the kids to help.

Heat the oil in a large wide skillet over medium-high heat until shimmering. Add the mushrooms and cook without disturbing for 4 to 6 minutes, until the mushrooms turn easily without sticking. Add the ginger, garlic, and cilantro stems and stir. Add the cabbage and carrots and stir again. Cover and wilt the cabbage for 5 minutes. Uncover, stir well, and add the mirin, soy sauce, and sesame oil. Bring to a boil, reduce the heat to medium, and add the peas and scallions. Cook until the liquid has cooked off and the filling is nearly dry, about 10 to 12 minutes longer. Stir in the cilantro leaves. Set the filling aside to cool completely.

Line a baking sheet with parchment paper. Place the sheet, the stack of wrappers, and the filling on the counter. Have a small bowl of cool water at hand. Taking one wrapper, dip your fingertip in the water, paint the edges, and place ¼ cup of the filling in the center. Tucking in the sides, roll the wrapper around the filling like a burrito. Place on the baking sheet and cover loosely with plastic wrap to keep the rolls from drying out. Continue to fill the wrappers until either the filling or the wrappers are gone.

(Continued)

Place a few layers of paper towel on a rack set over a baking sheet. In a straight-sided deep, heavy skillet, preferably cast iron, add about 2 inches of oil, at least ¾ inch below the rim of the pan. Heat the oil over medium-high heat to 375°F. In batches, slip in a few rolls, seam side down. The rolls will lower the temperature of the oil when they go into the pan, so adjust the heat accordingly, keeping the oil at 375°F to the best of your ability. Fry, staying vigilant and turning them as they become golden and blister, until browned and crispy all over and thoroughly cooked through, 7 to 9 minutes. Remove with a slotted spoon or spider and drain on the paper towels. Serve hot with the dipping sauce.

SWEET, SALTY, SPICY DIPPING SAUCE

Makes about ½ cup

¼ cup (60 ml) tamari or low-sodium soy sauce

¼ cup (60 ml) rice wine vinegar

1 tablespoon granulated sugar

1 teaspoon Sriracha or other hot sauce

1 tablespoon chopped cilantro

In a small bowl, stir together the tamari, vinegar, sugar, and Sriracha until the sugar has dissolved. Sprinkle the cilantro into the dipping sauce just before serving.

The sauce will keep, covered and refrigerated, for 4 days.

SAMOSA CIGARS

Makes about 21

¼ cup (15 g) finely chopped cilantro

2 tablespoons finely chopped onion

1 teaspoon grated ginger

1 medium garlic clove, grated

1 teaspoon lemon juice

¾ teaspoon coriander seeds, crushed

¾ teaspoon kosher salt, plus extra for the boiling water

½ teaspoon garam masala

¼ teaspoon cumin seeds, crushed

⅛ teaspoon cayenne

1 pound (450 g) Yukon Gold potatoes, peeled and cut into chunks

¼ cup (35 g) diced carrot

¼ cup (35 g) frozen peas

About 21 spring roll wrappers

2 to 3 cups (480 to 720 ml) grapeseed, peanut, or canola oil, for frying

---

Cilantro Chutney (page 53) or store-bought mango chutney, for serving (optional)

Samosas, those delicious fried treats, are most often made with a rolled dough, but I like to swap in store-bought spring roll wrappers for quick-to-the-table, satisfying, crunchy treats. Pleated at the ends like candy twisted in a pretty wrapper, they're a side dish for a cookout, a buffet table treat, or an easy way to use the leftover potatoes from last night's dinner. The spices are subtle and the layers of flavor create a sensational treat. Do not mash the potatoes until smooth—the nubby texture is essential.

In a medium bowl, combine the cilantro, onion, ginger, garlic, lemon juice, coriander, salt, garam masala, cumin, and cayenne.

Bring a medium saucepan of well-salted water to a boil over high heat. Add the potatoes and cook until fork tender, about 10 minutes. Remove the potatoes with a slotted spoon, shaking any excess water off before adding them to the onion and spices. Stir the diced carrot into the boiling water and cook for exactly 1 minute. With the slotted spoon, transfer to the bowl with the potatoes. Using a fork, combine the ingredients, leaving the texture a little chunky. Stir in the peas. Cool the filling to room temperature.

Line a baking sheet with parchment paper. Place the pan, the stack of wrappers, and the filling on the counter. Have a small bowl of cool water at hand. With your fingertip dipped in the water, paint the edges of one wrapper. Place 3 table-spoons of the potato filling along one edge of the wrapper, then roll it up like a cigar. Pinch the ends together firmly, using more water to make sure they pleat and stick together. Place on the baking sheet and cover loosely with plastic wrap to keep the cigars from drying out. Continue to fill the wrappers until either the filling or the wrappers are gone.

(Continued)

Samosa Cigars (page 201)

Chicken Tinga Half-Moons (page 204)

Place a few layers of paper towel on a rack set over a baking sheet. In a straight-sided deep heavy skillet, preferably cast iron, add about 2 inches of oil at least ¾ inch below the rim of the pan. Heat the oil over medium-high heat to 375°F. In batches, slip in a few cigars and fry, staying vigilant and turning them as they become golden and blister, until browned and crispy all over and thoroughly cooked through, 5 to 7 minutes. The rolls will lower the temperature of the oil when they first go into the pan, so adjust the heat accordingly, keeping the oil at 375°F to the best of your ability. Remove with tongs, a slotted spoon, or a spider and drain on the paper towels.

Serve hot with the chutney.

CHICKEN TINGA HALF-MOONS

Makes about 12

1 tablespoon grapeseed or canola oil

1 cup (142 g) finely chopped white onion

1 tablespoon grated garlic (about 2 cloves)

¾ cup (190 g) canned fire-roasted tomatoes (half a 15-ounce can)

¼ cup (60 ml) chicken stock or water

1 tablespoon adobo sauce from a can of chipotles in adobo, plus an optional chipotle, minced (see headnote)

1 teaspoon dried Mexican oregano or marjoram

½ teaspoon ground cumin

½ teaspoon kosher salt

1 cup (150 g) shredded or chopped cooked chicken

About 12 spring roll wrappers, cut into 5-inch rounds with a sharp cookie cutter (or use scissors)

¾ cup (142 g) chopped cabbage

¼ cup (56 g) shredded Monterey Jack cheese

About 2 cups (480 ml) grapeseed, peanut, or canola oil, for frying

Sizzling Salsa (recipe follows), for serving (optional)

Whether you roast a chicken regularly, or pick up a rotisserie chicken from the market, tinga is a pantry-friendly way of reimagining the familiar into another meal altogether. Tinga can be a tostada filling, a saucy taco filling, or, in this instance, a textured and tingling spicy mix enclosed in a crispy wrapper. The essential ingredient is the adobo sauce from a can of chipotles in adobo, found on most grocery shelves among the taco shells and enchilada sauces. The chipotle peppers themselves are up there on the Scoville heat index, so if you're spice-sensitive, or feeding this to a mixed crowd, omit the chipotle pepper in the filling, but be sure to make the Sizzling Salsa for the heat-seekers. One 15-ounce can of fire-roasted tomatoes is enough for both recipes.

Heat the oil in a large wide straight-sided skillet until shimmering. Stir in the onion and cook until wilted, about 4 minutes. Add the garlic, stir, and cook for only 30 seconds, then add the tomatoes, stock, adobo sauce, minced chipotle (if using), oregano, cumin, and salt. Simmer until the filling is thick and the liquid has cooked away, about 12 to 15 minutes. Stir in the chicken and set aside to cool completely.

Line a baking sheet with parchment paper. Place the sheet, the stack of wrappers, and the filling on the counter. Have a small bowl of cool water at hand. With your fingertip dipped in the water, paint the edge of one round. Place a scant ¼ cup filling in the center, followed by a generous tablespoon cabbage and about 2 teaspoons cheese. Fold into a half-moon, pressing to seal the edges. Place on the baking sheet and cover loosely with plastic wrap to keep them from drying out. Continue to fill the wrappers until either the filling or the wrappers are gone.

Place a few layers of paper towel on a rack set over a baking sheet. In a straight-sided deep heavy skillet, preferably cast iron, add about 2 inches of oil at least ¾ inch below the rim of the pan. Heat the oil over medium-high heat to 375°F. In batches, slip in two or three half-moons without crowding. The pies will lower the temperature of the oil when they go into the pan, so adjust the heat accordingly, keeping the oil at 375°F to the best of your ability. Fry, staying vigilant and turning them as they turn golden, blister, and puff up beautifully, until browned and crispy all over and thoroughly cooked through, about 5 minutes. Remove with a slotted spoon or spider and drain on the paper towels. Serve hot, with the salsa if you like.

SIZZLING SALSA

Makes 1 ½ cups

1 (1-inch-thick) slice of large white onion

1 whole garlic clove, peeled

¾ cup (190 g) canned fire-roasted tomatoes (half a 15-ounce can)

1 chipotle chile from a can of chipotles in adobo

¼ cup (30 g) salted peanuts

¼ cup (30 g) packed cilantro leaves and stems, plus extra for garnish

This salsa gets body and bulk from salted peanuts. It complements the Chicken Tinga Half-Moons, but it's also just terrific on a chip. There will be some left over, which is a very good thing. It lasts about 4 days in the refrigerator.

Blister the onion slice and garlic clove on an oiled griddle or well-seasoned cast-iron pan over high heat, or under the broiler. Let both sides pick up some dark brown, even blackened, spots. Transfer the onion and garlic to a blender and add the tomatoes, chipotle, peanuts, and cilantro. Blend until smooth. Scrape the salsa into a bowl, cover, and chill for 2 hours.

Bring to room temperature before serving. Garnish with a few fresh cilantro leaves before serving. May be made one day ahead.

Apple Funnel Cake Pie (page 209)

Strawberry Funnel Cake Pie

STRAWBERRY FUNNEL CAKE PIE

Makes 12

2 cups (335 g) chopped hulled fresh ripe strawberries

1 cup (142 g) chopped sweetened dried strawberries or other dried fruit

¼ cup (50 g) granulated sugar

2 teaspoons lemon juice

1 batch Buttermilk Dough for Fried Fruit Pies, page 267

2 to 3 cups canola or other neutral oil, for frying

Powdered sugar, for serving

If you've ever been to a county fair, perhaps you've nibbled on a hot, airy, tender funnel cake. It's not often I indulge, but there are times I think about the perfection of that first bite, the puff of heat, the tang, the sweet bite. It's what I want from a fried pie. To stiffen the filling, I add sweetened dried strawberries (see Resources, page 275), but golden raisins, dried cherries, and dried mango are all delicious options. You should be able to stretch the dough around the fruit so the pies will be plump and satisfying. Freeze them ahead, fry them to order, and serve warm, especially outside under the stars, with lightning bugs flickering in the hours after a summer cookout. Now, that's bliss.

Stir together the fresh strawberries, dried strawberries, sugar, and lemon juice in a small saucepan and bring to a boil over high heat, stirring all the time. Cook at a boil for about 12 minutes, until thick and jammy. Cool completely.

Bring the dough to room temperature at least 30 minutes before proceeding with the recipe. Place a few layers of paper towel on a rack set over a baking sheet. (Or use brown paper bags, which are excellent for draining!)

Line a baking sheet with parchment paper. Lightly dust the counter with flour and roll the dough to 16 by 12 inches, about ⅛ inch thick. Cut out 12 (4-inch) rounds. Place 2 tablespoons filling in the center of one. Lift the round carefully, by the edges, and keep the filling securely in the middle while you fold the round in half and press together the edges. Place the pie back down on the floured countertop and enthusiastically crimp the edge. Place on the parchment-lined baking sheet. Repeat until all the pies have been formed. Hold the pies in the freezer while the oil heats.

Heat 1 inch oil to 350°F in a straight-sided deep heavy skillet. I use a 10-inch cast-iron pan.

In batches of three, slide the pies into the hot oil and fry. The pies will lower the temperature of the oil when they go into the pan, so adjust the heat accordingly, keeping the oil at 350°F to the best of your ability. Watch as the pies blister and crackle and turn them every 30 seconds with a spider or slotted spoon to avoid scorching. Fry until golden brown, blistered, and crispy, about 3 minutes, then lift from the oil and drain on the paper towels. Continue to cook all the pies in this manner without crowding the pan.

Let the pies cool for a couple of minutes, then shower excessively with powdered sugar, and serve to everyone who has now gathered around. The filling will be very hot, so be careful.

APPLE FUNNEL CAKE PIE

Makes 12

1½ cups (170 g) chopped peeled crisp tart apples like Gala or Pink Lady (2 medium)

⅓ cup (70 g) packed brown sugar

2 tablespoons fresh lemon juice

¾ teaspoon ground cinnamon

¾ cup (42 g) dried apples, chopped

1 batch Buttermilk Dough for Fried Fruit Pies, page 267

2 to 3 cups canola or other neutral oil, for frying

Powdered sugar

According to Ronni Lundy, the author of *Victuals*, a beautifully written cookbook filled with stories of the foods of the Mountain South, fried pies are an Appalachian-born treat always made with dried apples. Across the mountains of Virginia, Tennessee, and North Carolina, generations have sliced fall apples and dried them on a tin roof. Look for dried apples that are plump and flexible, often found at health food stores. I spied some at my farmers' market, dried by the apple grower himself. When I asked, he said it's something his family has done for generations—without a dehydrator!

Stir together the fresh apple, brown sugar, lemon juice, and cinnamon in a small saucepan. Bring to a boil over high heat, stirring all the time. Cook at a boil for about 8 minutes, until the apples have started to soften. Stir in the dried apples and cool completely.

Bring the dough to room temperature at least 30 minutes before proceeding with the recipe. Place a few layers of paper towel on a rack set over a baking sheet.

Lightly dust the counter with flour and roll the dough to 16 by 12 inches, about ⅛ inch thick. Cut out 12 (4-inch) rounds. Place 2 tablespoons filling in the center of one round. Lift the round carefully, by the edges, and keep the filling securely in the middle while you fold the round in half and press together the edges. Place the pie back down on the floured countertop and enthusiastically crimp the edge with a floured table fork. Repeat until all the pies have been formed.

Heat 1 inch of oil to 350°F in a straight-sided deep heavy skillet. I use a 10-inch cast-iron pan.

In batches of three, slide the pies into the hot oil without

(Continued)

crowding the pan. The pies will lower the temperature of the oil when they go into the pan, so adjust the heat accordingly, keeping the oil at 350°F to the best of your ability. Watch as they blister and crackle, turning the pies every 30 seconds with long-handled tongs, a spider, or a slotted spoon to avoid scorching. Fry until the pies are golden brown, blistered, and crispy, about 3 minutes, then lift from the oil and place on the paper towels to drain. Continue to cook all the pies in this manner.

Let the pies cool for a couple of minutes, shower excessively with powdered sugar, and serve to everyone who has now gathered around. The filling will be very hot, so be careful.

CHAPTER 8

KOLACHE

FILLED BUNS BY WAY OF EASTERN EUROPE

Spicy and savory or sweet and streuseled, kolache are satisfying, pillowy, yeasted buns that originated in Eastern Europe and are now at home across Texas, Nebraska, and parts of Wisconsin and Minnesota.

n most of eastern Europe, *kolache* is a very general term referring to a sweet dough pastry. To further confuse the matter, *kolach* also means cookie; and that plural is *kolachki*. (There is no such word as *kolaches*.) These days, and in our current vernacular, wrong as it might be, *kolache* refers broadly to an enriched soft bun, about the size of a softball, that is shaped and filled in a number of different ways, all regionally defined. Traditional fillings run from apricot (page 221) to prune, poppy to sweet cheese (page 226), to almost any thick fruit jam (like pineapple, page 224).

In the 19th century, Czechoslovakian immigrants in Texas established a kolache with typical Texas flair, filled with sausage, chiles, and cheese (page 219). Texas has claimed kolache as their own, but you'll find other versions of kolache throughout Nebraska, Minnesota, Wisconsin, Iowa, and other communities where Eastern European immigrants settled. Look for them at festivals, occasionally in bakeries, and frequently at markets and bake sales.

SAY IT WITH ME: KO-LASCH

Kolache dough is yeasty and bouncy, with a tender, tight crumb. If I have time, I like to ferment the yeast dough overnight, not only to deepen the flavor but to make wrestling the dough into shape easier than with a freshly risen balloon. Make the dough after dinner and have breakfast buns in the morning. The recipe for the basic enriched, yeast-raised dough can be found on page 269.

MAKING KOLACHE

The shape and form of a kolache offers potential for internecine feuding. Beyond the rounded, filled bun, which turned out to be my favorite shape, kolache are sometimes flat cookies folded like an envelope. There are flat round kolache, looking just like breakfast Danish, with filling and streusel on top. Some places make kolache in a buttered, parchment-lined 9- by 13-inch deep baking dish, so the square pull-apart buns touch each other at their soft, pillowy sides and have a divot of sweet jammy fruit on the surface. I even found a recipe for a pizza-size kolache with eight defined slices—each with a different jammy filling—with carefully pleated and pinched dough

dividing the round into generous servings: family-size and family-style. For the purposes of the following recipes, I've focused on rounded buns with filling in the center and, for the sweet varieties, the addition of streusel on top.

Making the dough (page 269) is straightforward: With all ingredients added to the stand mixer at once, the dough hook does the work and a ball of velvety goodness is ready to rise. Tip the dough into a well-oiled bowl and, in just 1 hour, it will be blousy and full of air bubbles. Alternatively, proof the dough overnight, or for up to 16 hours, in the refrigerator. Bring the dough back to room temperature (about an hour) before proceeding.

Kolache dough is springy and satiny. It feels great in the hand and promises a lovely, tender bun. But don't be fooled. Stay on course. Keep track. Do not let the dough rise for more than the intended time. The dough has two very significant deflations and will bounce back. Overproofing is your enemy. Too much time rising and the buns will spring in the oven and grow bulbous and then slightly collapse when they cool.

In addition, over-proofing may cause a space to form between the filling and the bun, also making the kolache more likely to collapse on the top. Even if they do crater, they're still thoroughly delightful and positively delicious; they just don't look as perfect. If you are not able to be timely with the second rise, chill the buns before baking to retard the proofing, but for no more than 30 minutes.

STORING KOLACHE

These pastries stale very quickly; plan to serve them shortly after baking. Or, once cool, wrap in foil to store for a day or two in the refrigerator;   leave them wrapped to reheat in a 350°F oven for about 10 minutes. The toaster oven was made for this.

It's also possible to freeze the cooled pastries and reheat as needed. Individually wrap them well in foil, then place in a ziptop bag and freeze. To serve, heat the kolache, still frozen and wrapped in the foil, in a 350°F oven for about 25 minutes. Use a toaster oven if you have one.

HATCH CHILE, CORN, AND COTIJA KOLACHE

Makes 12

1 recipe Enriched Yeast Dough for Kolache, page 269

About 1 tablespoon grapeseed or canola oil

4 to 6 (10 ounces, 285 g) tomatillos, husk removed and halved

1 small white onion (5 ounces, 140 g), peeled and halved

2 garlic cloves, smashed and peeled

¼ cup (4 ounces, 113 g) canned chopped Hatch or jalapeño chiles, drained

¼ cup (15 g) chopped cilantro

2 tablespoons freshly squeezed lime juice

1 teaspoon dried Mexican oregano or marjoram

½ teaspoon kosher salt

1 cup (180 g) fresh or frozen corn kernels

½ cup (56 g) crumbled cotija or feta cheese

Egg wash (1 egg beaten with 1 tablespoon cool water and ¼ teaspoon kosher salt)

It didn't seem fair for my vegetarian friends that so many of the savory kolache are meaty, so I made a vegetarian kolache that even a carnivore could love. The tomatillo filling is spiked with bright, acidic Hatch chiles and bulked up with corn and nuggets of salty cotija. Hatch chiles are sometimes called New Mexico chiles. For this recipe, canned chiles are perfect; small cans of Hatch chiles can be found in the Latin food aisle of most grocery stores. Substitute chopped green chiles, if necessary.

Bring the dough to room temperature 1 hour before proceeding with the recipe.

Heat a cast-iron skillet over high heat and skim the surface of the pan with oil. Place the tomatillos flesh side up in the skillet and quickly sear and char the skin, about 4 minutes. Remove the tomatillos and place in the jar of a blender. Add another skim of oil to the pan, then add the onion halves, cut side down, and the garlic and stir quickly to blacken the edges here and there, just a minute or two. Add to the blender and whir until the mixture is smooth.

Return the mixture to the skillet and cook over medium-high heat until reduced by half, about 12 minutes. Stir in the chiles, cilantro, lime juice, oregano, and salt and cook for another 2 to 3 minutes, until thick and combined. Spoon in the corn kernels and stir to combine. Let cool. Add the cheese, then cover and refrigerate until ready to use. The filling will keep for a week.

Line two baking sheets with parchment. Generously flour the work surface. Tip the dough onto the work surface and press down firmly to deflate. Divide the dough into 12 equal pieces (85 to 95 grams each). Flour the dough very well. Flatten each piece into a disk about the size of a saucer, keeping the center thick and the edge thinner.

Hold one dough disk across the palm of one hand and place 3 tablespoons chile filling in the center. Pull in the edges to form a globe about the size of a lemon, then firmly pinch together the edges. Set the kolache seam side down on the floured counter and gently roll the dough lightly under the rounded palm of the hand to form a tight ball. Check the seam, pinch again if necessary, and place on one prepared baking sheet. Repeat with the remaining pieces of dough, placing them about 1 inch apart on the two sheets. Brush the tops with the egg wash. Cover with plastic wrap and place in a warm, draft-free place to rise until puffy, about 15 minutes.

Heat the oven to 350°F. Slide the baking sheets onto the oven's center rack and bake for 15 to 20 minutes, until the kolache are golden brown. If the oven will not accommodate both baking sheets on one rack, place one in the refrigerator and bake the two trays sequentially. Serve while still warm.

TEXAS-STYLE SAUSAGE AND JALAPEÑO BREAKFAST KOLACHE

Makes 12

1 recipe Enriched Yeast Dough for Kolache, page 269

1 teaspoon grapeseed or canola oil, plus more if needed

½ pound (225 g) breakfast sausage, bulk or removed from the casings

½ cup (70 g) ½-inch diced red onion

5 large eggs, lightly beaten

¼ cup (30 g) chopped fresh chives

½ teaspoon kosher salt

3 ounces (84 g) pepper Jack or Monterey Jack cheese, shredded (about ¾ cup)

12 pickled jalapeño slices (optional)

Egg wash (1 egg beaten with 1 tablespoon cool water and ¼ teaspoon kosher salt)

Flaky salt for sprinkling

Regional versions of the breakfast sandwich thrill me. When I travel, I look for any form of bacon-egg-cheese (BEC) or its cousin, the sausage-egg-cheese (SEC), to get my morning engine started. While in some parts of Texas the breakfast taco rules, in other places a great on-the-go breakfast (or sit-down-and-savor-it breakfast) is the tender egg and meat kolache. The pickled jalapeño kicks this right into Deliciousville, so while the ingredient list shows it as optional, in my mind it is mandatory.

Bring the dough to room temperature 1 hour before proceeding with the recipe.

Heat a skillet over medium-high heat and add the oil. Scatter in the sausage meat and cook and stir until the pink is just gone, 8 to 10 minutes. Remove the meat and spread on a baking sheet to cool.

Add the red onion to the pan (and 1 tablespoon oil, if needed) and cook over medium heat until tender, about 5 minutes. Stir in the eggs, chives, and salt. Cook quickly and gently, tossing the mixture until the eggs are almost cooked through, but still a little runny. Scrape this mixture onto the baking sheet with the sausage, spreading it out to cool rapidly. When cool, stir the meat, onions, eggs, and cheese together. The filling can be covered and refrigerated for up to a day.

Line two baking sheets with parchment. Generously flour the work surface. Tip the dough onto the work surface and press down firmly to deflate. Divide the dough into 12 equal pieces (85 to 95 grams each). Flour the counter and the dough very well. Flatten each piece of dough into a disk about the size of a saucer, keeping the center thick and the edge thinner.

Hold a dough disk across the palm of one hand and place 3 tablespoons filling in the center, then top with one jalapeño slice, if using. Pull in the edges to form a globe about the size of a lemon and firmly pinch together the edges. Set the kolache seam side down on the floured counter and gently roll the dough lightly under the rounded palm of the hand to form a tight ball. Check the seam, pinch again if necessary, then place on one prepared baking sheet. Repeat with the remaining pieces of dough, placing them about 1 inch apart on the two sheets. Brush the tops with the egg wash and sprinkle with a few grains of flaky salt. Cover loosely with a clean tea towel or plastic wrap and place in a warm, draft-free place to rise until puffy, about 15 minutes.

Heat the oven to 350°F. Slide the baking sheets onto the oven's center rack and bake for 15 to 20 minutes, until the kolache are golden brown. If the oven will not accommodate both baking sheets on one rack, place one in the refrigerator and bake the two trays sequentially. Serve while still warm.

APRICOT KOLACHE

Makes 12

1 recipe Enriched
Yeast Dough for
Kolache, page 269

---

9 ounces (256 g)
dried apricots,
finely chopped

1 cup (240 ml)
water

1 cup (200 g)
granulated sugar

¼ cup (60 ml)
fresh orange juice,
warmed

½ cup (60 g)
all-purpose flour

4 tablespoons
(56 g) unsalted
butter, softened

Egg wash
(1 egg beaten
with 1 tablespoon
cool water and
¼ teaspoon
kosher salt)

This classic filling is jammy and not too sweet. Use plump dried apricots, fresh and tangy, for the best results; if chopping them into little bits seems like too much work, use the food processor to finely chop them with the sugar. I like to combine the apricot and sweet cheese (page 226) fillings for a sweet and tart breakfast combo.

Bring the dough to room temperature 1 hour before proceeding with the recipe.

Combine the chopped apricots and water in a small saucepan over high heat. Bring to a boil and cook, stirring continually, until the liquid has nearly evaporated but the fruit is still loose and manageable. Remove from the heat and stir in ½ cup of the sugar and the juice. Let cool.

To make the streusel, combine the flour and remaining ½ cup sugar, then work in the butter with your fingertips until crumbly. Set aside.

Line two baking sheets with parchment. Generously flour the work surface. Tip the dough onto the work surface and press down firmly to deflate. Divide the dough into 12 equal pieces (85 to 95 grams each). Flour the dough very well. Flatten each piece of dough into a disk about the size of a saucer, keeping the center thick and the edge thinner.

Hold one dough disk across the palm of one hand and place 3 tablespoons apricot filling in the center. Pull in the edges to form a globe about the size of a lemon, then firmly pinch together the edges. Set the kolache seam side down on the floured counter and gently roll the dough lightly under the rounded palm of the hand to form a tight ball. Check the seam, pinch again if necessary, and place on one prepared baking sheet. Repeat with the remaining pieces of dough, placing them about 1 inch apart on the two sheets. Brush

the tops with the egg wash and cover with a generous 2 tablespoons streusel. Cover with plastic wrap and place in a warm, draft-free place to rise until puffy, about 15 minutes.

Heat the oven to 350°F. Slide the baking sheets onto the oven's center rack and bake for 15 to 20 minutes, until the kolache are golden brown. If the oven will not accommodate both baking sheets on one rack, place one in the refrigerator and bake the two trays sequentially. Serve while still warm.

PINEAPPLE AND TOASTED COCONUT KOLACHE

Makes 12

1 recipe Enriched Yeast Dough for Kolache, page 269

2 cups (340 g) fresh, peeled, and cored pineapple, cut into ½-inch dice (from a 3-pound medium pineapple, with some left over)

1 cup (213 g) packed brown sugar

1¼ cups (140 g) plus ⅓ cup (35 g) unsweetened shredded coconut, toasted

2 tablespoons spiced rum, like Myers's (optional)

⅛ teaspoon kosher salt

⅓ cup (40 g) all-purpose flour

⅓ cup (65 g) granulated sugar

3 tablespoons (42 g) unsalted butter, softened

Egg wash (1 egg beaten with 1 tablespoon cool water and ¼ teaspoon kosher salt)

Fruit-filled kolache are common—most often apricot or prune. While those flavors are positively delicious, I love the flavor of slow-cooked pineapple, particularly when tinged with a bit of spiced rum. Add some coconut for texture, and this kolache feels as delicious as the breeze from swaying palm trees.

Bring the dough to room temperature 1 hour before proceeding with the recipe.

Combine the diced pineapple and brown sugar in a small saucepan over high heat. Bring to a boil and cook, stirring continually, until the liquid has nearly evaporated but the filling is still loose and manageable, about 15 to 20 minutes. Remove from the heat and stir in the 1¼ cups (140 g) coconut, the rum (if using), and salt.

To make the streusel, combine the flour, granulated sugar, and remaining ⅓ cup (35 g) coconut, then work in the butter with your fingertips until crumbly.

Line two baking sheets with parchment. Generously flour the work surface. Tip the dough onto the work surface and press down firmly to deflate. Divide the dough into 12 equal pieces (85 to 95 grams each). Flour the dough very well. Flatten each piece of dough into a disk about the size of a saucer, keeping the center thick and the edge thinner.

Hold one dough disk across the palm of one hand and place 3 tablespoons pineapple filling in the center. Pull in the edges to form a globe about the size of a lemon and firmly pinch together the edges. Set the kolache seam side down on the floured counter and gently roll the dough lightly under the rounded palm of the hand to form a tight ball. Check

the seam, pinch again if necessary, and place on one pre-pared baking sheet. Repeat with the remaining pieces of dough, placing them about 1 inch apart on the two sheets. Brush the tops with the egg wash and cover with a generous 2 tablespoons streusel. Cover with plastic wrap and place in a warm, draft-free place to rise until puffy, about 15 minutes.

Heat the oven to 350°F. Slide the baking sheets onto the oven's center rack and bake for 15 to 20 minutes, until the kolache are golden brown. If the oven will not accommodate both baking sheets on one rack, place one in the refrigerator and bake the two trays sequentially. Serve while still warm.

SWEET CHEESE KOLACHE

Makes 12

1 recipe Enriched
Yeast Dough for
Kolache, page 269

½ cup (125 g)
farmer's cheese
(or substitute
drained ricotta
cheese, see
headnote)

12 tablespoons
(6 ounces, 170 g)
cream cheese,
softened

3 tablespoons
powdered sugar

1 large egg yolk

½ teaspoon vanilla
extract

Pinch of kosher
salt

½ cup (60 g)
all-purpose flour

½ cup (100 g)
granulated sugar

¼ cup (30 g)
chopped almonds

1 teaspoon
ground cinnamon

4 tablespoons
(56 g) softened
butter

Egg wash
(1 egg beaten
with 1 tablespoon
cool water and
¼ teaspoon
kosher salt)

Given a choice, cheese Danish are my very favorite, so it was no surprise that I fell in love with the idea of kolache bursting with a sweet cheese filling reminiscent of Danish and blintzes and sweet noodle kugel. The ideal cheese for this filling is farmer's cheese, but it's harder and harder to find these days, so if it's not available where you are, drain ricotta (in a sieve set over a bowl) for several hours to remove as much of the moisture as possible. If it still seems wet, press on the surface to squeeze out more moisture. The cream cheese stabilizes the filling to keep it from seeping into the kolache dough, so it must be thoroughly blended with the ricotta to do its work, and the ricotta needs to be as dry as possible.

Bring the dough to room temperature 1 hour before proceeding with the recipe.

Use a stand mixer, hand mixer, or whisk to combine the farmer's cheese, cream cheese, powdered sugar, egg yolk, vanilla, and salt until smooth and creamy.

To make the streusel, combine the flour, granulated sugar, almonds, and cinnamon, then work in the butter with your fingertips until crumbly.

Line two baking sheets with parchment. Generously flour the work surface. Tip the dough onto the work surface and press down firmly to deflate. Divide the dough into 12 equal pieces (85 to 95 grams each). Flour the dough very well. Flatten each piece of dough into a disk about the size of a saucer, keeping the center thick and the edge thinner.

Hold one dough disk across the palm of one hand and place 3 tablespoons cheese filling in the center. Pull in the edges to form a globe about the size of a lemon, then firmly pinch together the edges. Set the kolache seam side down on the floured counter and gently roll the dough lightly under the rounded palm of the hand to form a tight ball. Check the seam, pinch again if necessary, then place on one prepared baking sheet. Repeat with the remaining pieces of dough, placing them about 1 inch apart on the two sheets. Brush the tops with the egg wash and cover with a generous 2 tablespoons streusel. Cover with plastic wrap and place in a warm, draft-free place to rise until puffy, about 15 minutes.

Heat the oven to 350°F. Slide the baking sheets onto the oven's center rack and bake for 15 to 20 minutes, until the kolache are golden brown. If the oven will not accommodate both baking sheets on one rack, place one in the refrigerator and bake the two trays sequentially. Serve while still warm.

VARIATION

For each kolache, place a teaspoon of raspberry, cherry, or apricot jam on the dough before spooning on the cheese filling, and then form the kolache.

CHAPTER 9

KNISHES

DELI CASE PIES

Forget what you think a knish is all about—those leaden beasts on street carts are not representative. A knish is snacky and satisfying, with whisper-thin layers of pastry wrapped around a rich filling. A knish is just the right size to battle the midafternoon hungries.

knish is a plump, filled, crackly pastry. Because it's traditional in many Jewish homes, the dough, page 271, is specifically made with no butter or other dairy products, meaning it can be used to wrap up either meat or dairy fillings (as kosher households do not mix the two). Classic knishes are filled with potatoes, onions, ground meat, or cheese. While they can be baked or fried, I've opted for a baked version here. My knishes are also quite a bit smaller than what's usually served. Have another if you're still hungry (said in my grandmother's voice).

AN OILY DOUGH

Knish dough is unlike any of the other doughs in this book. It's weirdly oily and seems destined to be a problem. Instead, once it rests for a while, it rolls out and stretches easily. Holes are no big deal; just pinch the dough together and carry on. Making knishes is a forgiving, fun, filled-pastry project, another in the line of great leftover concepts from around the world.

Opt for schmaltz (rendered chicken, duck, or goose fat) or vegetable oil as the fat for this dough. Either is traditional. Choose any oil from peanut to corn oil to grapeseed or Wesson. Olive oil has too strong a flavor, and nut oils will burn.

Tip the dough out of the bowl onto the counter. There is no need for flour; it won't stick. Knead the dough again to make it malleable and take up any oil that was in the bottom of the bowl.

FORMING KNISHES

Divide the dough into three pieces, put two of the pieces back in the bowl and keep covered. Roll one piece of the dough to a 12-inch square. It will be whisper thin. I prefer to use a rolling pin, but you can stretch the dough to size, as you might with Pulled Dough for Strudel (page 262)—it's very malleable. Leaving a border of about an inch on the edge closest to you, place 1 cup of filling along the length of the dough, forming a log. Lift the edge of the dough up and over the filling—this is when the dough is likely to develop a hole or two. Don't worry one bit. Just keep on rolling it up until you reach the other edge. Pinch the long seam to seal and do the same if there are any holes. The "log" may be a little lumpy; that's okay.

If you've ever made sausages, forming knishes requires the same set of actions. With the log in front of you, use the side of your hand to make five evenly spaced indents along the roll, forming six even segments. Grasping the log, form each knish by slightly twisting at the indents in opposite directions. Voila, six pudgy, little knishes!

Use scissors or a pizza wheel to slice the pastries apart. Knishes can be made with an open top, very handy if serving differently filled knishes so the filling is exposed, or all closed up and contained. The dough is stretchy, so either option is possible. One end of each knish will inevitably have more pastry, so start by tucking and pinching the dough at that end to make a flat bottom. Place the knish down on the counter and pull and stretch the dough up over the top, either exposing a bit of the filling, or pinching it together until the top is closed and looks like, as my grandmother would say, a *pupik,* a belly button. Work in this way to form six round, tidy, snug little bundles.

Place the knishes on a parchment-lined baking sheet and repeat with the other two segments of dough until 18 knishes are on the sheet. Brush with egg wash and bake at 375°F until golden brown, usually around 30 minutes.

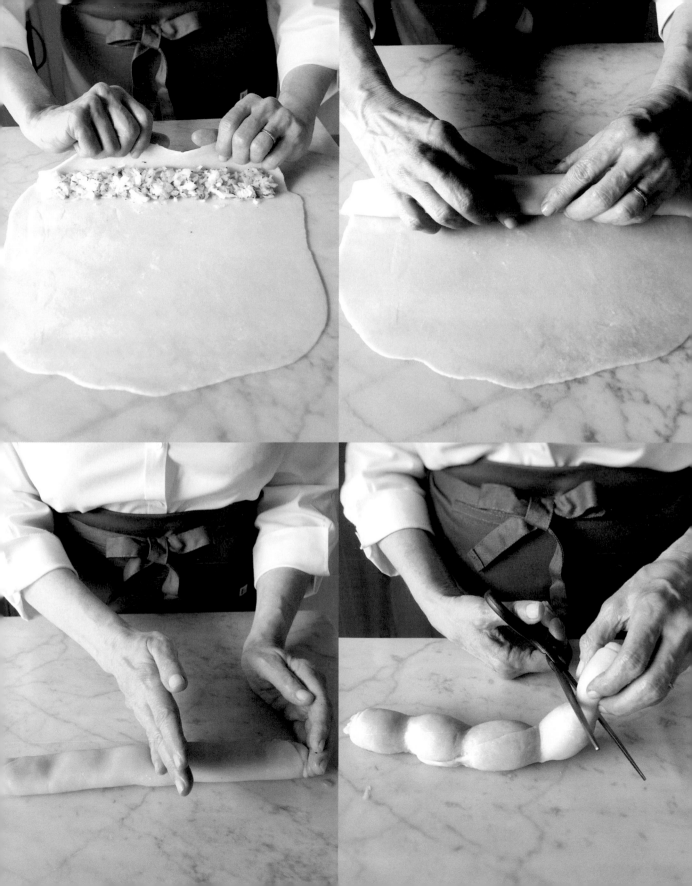

CLASSIC POTATO KNISHES

Makes 18 small knishes

1¾ pounds (800 g)
russet potatoes
(about 4 medium)

¾ cup (180 g)
crème fraîche

4 tablespoons
(56 g) unsalted
butter

¼ cup (15 g)
snipped chives

¼ cup (15 g) finely
chopped fresh
flat-leaf parsley

1 teaspoon
kosher salt

½ teaspoon
freshly ground
black pepper

1 batch Dairy-
Free Dough for
Knishes, page 271

Egg wash
(1 egg beaten
with 1 tablespoon
cool water and
¼ teaspoon
kosher salt)

Wrap silky, creamy mashed potatoes in a thin, crackly knish pastry and hear the angels sing. Go on, it's carb-on-carb time. Use a fork to fluff up the taters before stirring in generous lashings of butter and crème fraîche. My grandmother did not know from crème fraîche. When I found her recipe card for potato knishes, she calls for farmer's cheese or cottage cheese, no doubt because she had my grandfather on a perpetual diet. Feel free to swap in sour cream, yogurt, cream cheese, or cottage cheese.

Heat the oven to 350°F. Scrub the potatoes and pierce them with a sharp knife in three or four places. Bake on the oven rack for 55 to 60 minutes, until a fork glides easily into the center. Remove from the oven and, holding a hot potato with a towel, make a vertical slit across the top. Squeeze at both ends to open the potatoes and release the steam. Use a fork to fluff the potato, then scrape it away from the peel and add to a generous bowl. Add the crème fraîche, butter, chives, parsley, salt, and pepper to the potatoes and stir and mash with a fork, a potato masher, or sturdy whisk and a strong arm. The texture of the filling may be chunky or smooth—either is delicious. To make it silky smooth, use the stand mixer and the whisk attachment to whip the ingredients. Cool completely.

Heat the oven to 375°F. Line two baking sheets with parchment. Knead the dough and divide into three pieces. Roll out one piece to a 12-inch square, add 1 cup filling in a log on one end, and roll up. Form six even segments (like making sausage), cut between them to make separate pastries, then form into six knishes. (See Forming Knishes, page 230.) Repeat to make 18 knishes.

Brush with egg wash and bake until golden brown, usually around 30 minutes. Serve warm.

TOP TO BOTTOM:

Onion and Sauerkraut Knish (page 234)
Classic Potato Knish (page 232)
Veal and Mushroom Knish (page 237)
Spicy Lamb, Almond, and Raisin Knish (page 238)

ONION AND SAUERKRAUT KNISHES

Makes 18 small knishes

2 tablespoons olive oil

4 cups (570 g) ½-inch diced onion (about 4 medium)

2 cups (220 g) chopped drained sauerkraut

1 teaspoon freshly ground black pepper

1 teaspoon caraway seed

Salt, only if needed

---

1 recipe Dairy-Free Dough for Knishes, page 271

Egg wash (1 egg beaten with 1 tablespoon cool water and ¼ teaspoon kosher salt)

Onion and sauerkraut is a classic combination found in Eastern Europe's *pierogies* and *varnishkes*, *pelmeni*, and knishes. It's not a surprise, considering the limited winter larders in those northern climates, but what may be surprising is the absolutely thrilling peppery, salty, sour, and sweet combination. The trick is cooking the onions gently and slowly to bring out their intrinsically sweet flavor, a very gentle caramelization. If they blacken, the filling will be bitter. It's a razor's edge, I tell you!

Heat the oil in a large wide skillet over medium-high heat until it shimmers. Add the onions in an even layer and cook, stirring occasionally, until they are golden brown with some pieces a little darker than golden, about 15 to 20 minutes. Scrape the onions into a bowl and stir in the sauerkraut, pepper, and caraway seed. Taste and add salt if needed. Cool completely.

Heat the oven to 375°F. Line two baking sheets with parchment.

Knead the dough and divide into three pieces. Roll out one piece to a 12-inch square, add 1 cup filling in a log on one end, and roll up. Form six even segments (like making sausage), cut between them to make separate pastries, then form into six knishes. (See Forming Knishes, page 230, for complete instructions.) Repeat to make 18 knishes.

Brush with egg wash and bake until golden brown, usually around 30 minutes. Serve warm.

CLOCKWISE, FROM TOP LEFT, FILLINGS FOR KNISHES: Veal and Mushroom Knish (page 237);
Spicy Lamb, Almond, and Raisin Knish (page 238); Onion and Sauerkraut Knish (page 234);
Classic Potato Knish (page 232)

VEAL AND MUSHROOM KNISHES

Makes 18 small knishes

1 tablespoon olive oil

4 ounces (110 g) cremini mushrooms (about 6), stemmed and sliced thin

½ cup (70 g) diced onion

1 pound (450 g) ground veal

1 teaspoon minced garlic

½ cup (70 g) diced carrot

1 teaspoon sweet paprika

½ teaspoon dried oregano

1 teaspoon kosher salt

½ teaspoon freshly ground black pepper

2 cups (450 g) canned crushed tomatoes

1 batch Dairy-Free Dough for Knishes, page 271

Egg wash (1 egg beaten with 1 tablespoon cool water and ¼ teaspoon kosher salt)

If ever a knish deserved a glass of red wine, this is it. Veal and mushrooms come together in a goulash way, a stewy combo that reminds me of a regular meal at my great-grandmother's house. Rich and meaty, but not at all heavy. While there were many reasons to eschew veal in the past, animal husbandry has come a long way when it comes to humane production. Look for pink veal, or veal raised on grass or grain, a sign of a very thoughtful farmer.

Heat the oil in a large wide skillet over high heat until it shimmers. Add the mushrooms and cook, shaking the pan and pan-roasting the mushrooms, until golden brown, about 6 minutes. Add the onion and cook until it's wilted, about 4 minutes more. Add the ground veal and cook, breaking it apart with two wooden spoons until there are no large chunks of meat and no pink remaining. Stir in the garlic, cook for 30 seconds, then stir in the carrot, paprika, oregano, salt, and pepper. Add the tomatoes and cook, uncovered, for 20 to 25 minutes, stirring here and there, until the filling is still moist but not at all soupy. It should not be sticking to the pan. Cool completely.

Heat the oven to 375°F. Line two baking sheets with parchment.

Knead the dough and divide into three pieces. Roll out one piece to a 12-inch square, add 1 cup filling in a log on one end, and roll up. Form six even segments (like making sausage), cut between them to make separate pastries, then form into six knishes. (See Forming Knishes, page 230, for complete instructions.) Repeat to make 18 knishes.

Brush with egg wash and bake until golden brown, usually around 30 minutes. Serve warm.

SPICY LAMB, ALMOND, AND RAISIN KNISHES

Makes 18 small knishes

¼ cup (60 ml) fino (dry) sherry

½ cup (85 g) golden raisins

1 tablespoon grapeseed or canola oil

1 pound (450 g) ground lamb

1 tablespoon harissa

1 tablespoon Ras al Hanout (recipe follows)

1 teaspoon smoked paprika

1 teaspoon kosher salt

½ cup (57 g) slivered almonds, toasted

---

1 batch Dairy-Free Dough for Knishes, page 271

Egg wash (1 egg beaten with 1 tablespoon cool water and ¼ teaspoon kosher salt)

Spicy, sweet, salty, and crunchy, a knish benefits from a complex filling, and this Moroccan-themed lamb fits the bill. Make sure the meat is cooked through and not too chunky to avoid lumpy knishes. If your gathering includes raisin-haters, omit the fruit and carry on.

Gently heat the sherry in a small saucepan, but do not boil. Turn off the heat, add the raisins, cover, and let steep for 15 minutes. Heat the oil in a large, wide skillet over medium-high heat until it shimmers. Add the lamb and cook, breaking it apart with two wooden spoons, until there is no pink remaining and no large chunks. Do not pour off fat that has accumulated in the pan; without it, the filling will be dry. Stir in the harissa, ras al hanout, paprika, and salt. Add the raisins with the sherry, stir, and cook for 30 seconds. Remove from the heat, stir in the almonds, and cool completely.

Heat the oven to 375°F. Line two baking sheets with parchment.

Knead the dough and divide into three pieces. Roll out one piece to a 12-inch square, add 1 cup filling in a log on one end, and roll up. Form six even segments (like making sausage), cut between them to make separate pastries, then form into six knishes. (See Forming Knishes, page 230, for complete instructions.) Repeat to make 18 knishes.

Brush with egg wash and bake until golden brown, usually around 30 minutes. Serve warm.

RAS AL HANOUT

Makes about 1 ½ tablespoons

½ teaspoon
black pepper

½ teaspoon
ground ginger

¼ teaspoon
ground cumin

½ teaspoon
ground cinnamon

¼ teaspoon
ground coriander

¼ teaspoon
cayenne

Scant ⅛ teaspoon
ground cloves

Ras al hanout, a spice blend used in Moroccan and other North African countries, is piquant and nuanced and full of flavor. Sprinkle it on a tomato and cucumber salad with feta cheese.

In a small jar, mix the pepper, ginger, cumin, cinnamon, coriander, cayenne, and cloves. Keep tightly covered.

CHAPTER 10

FEARLESS PIE AND PASTRY DOUGHS

Pie and pastry doughs don't have to be difficult or dramatic. Here are straightforward and forgiving recipes where practice is the essential ingredient. Be kind to yourself as you learn to make pies fly.

THE PIE DOUGHS

For galettes, tarts, hand pies, pie poppers, and empanadas, the following techniques and recipes rely on my have-no-fear food processor method, turning out perfect pie dough time after time.

WEIGHING

Dear readers, I'm going to say it again: Please use a scale. Having a digital kitchen scale in easy reach gives you a leg up on success. Weight is always more consistent than volume measures, and the results will be, too. Flour is an especially wily ingredient, easily stuffed inside a cup measure, and if packed too tight could be almost one and a half times as much as a recipe calls for.

If precision doesn't convince you, maybe dishwashing will. If you start with one bowl (the work bowl from the food processor or the stand mixer, for instance), and weigh and add each ingredient, setting the scale to zero between each addition, there will be no bowls to wash, no sticky cup measures. Just the work bowl. That's got to be a win.

So, please, get a kitchen scale (see Resources, page 275). Put it on the counter or keep it inside a convenient drawer and make taking it out part of the preparations for baking. Soon it will be second nature.

MIXING

Pie dough is made up of flour, fat, and cold liquid. A perfect pie dough will roll out easily without smearing or fighting back. It will crimp, lattice, and take to cutouts without any issue. And it will emerge from the oven golden brown and crispy, layered, and flavorful. I like to watch people as they taste my pie for the first time. They smile. Pie should make everyone smile.

When making pie dough, speed and temperature are most important. The success of the pie depends on organizing the ingredients, then mixing, wrapping, and chilling the dough quickly.

There are three ways to mix pie dough: with a food processor, by hand, and (only in a pinch) with a stand mixer. My hands-down favorite is the food processor. In fact, pie crust may be the primary reason I own a food processor. Nothing "cuts in" butter better. It also makes quick work of grating vegetables, mixing up scone and biscuit dough, and slicing mushrooms for gravy. But I digress.

The recipes in this book are written for the food processor. But you can use either of the other two methods with confidence. The dough that emerges is the same whether made in a machine or with your hands. But the food processor is fast and absolutely consistent and that's why I like it. Less than 2 minutes and you've got pie dough, wrapped and ready for the refrigerator.

Mixing Pie Dough with a Food Processor

The food processor method is the default method in the following dough recipes. Be sure to use a processor with a 7-cup or larger capacity, not a mini processor. Place the processor work bowl on the scale and tare (zero) the weight. Add flour to the bowl until it reaches the desired weight. Then tare again and weigh in the cold cubed butter, and then add the salt. Move the bowl to the food processor and use the Pulse function to cut the butter into the flour until it is pebbly with nuggets of butter throughout. Add the cold liquid all at once and process until the dough almost comes together in a rough ball. You'll hear the sounds change to *chunka chunka chunka* as the gathered clump hits

Weigh. Pulse. Incorporate.

the side of the bowl. All the flour will be dampened and the dough will be a shaggy clump. Scrape the processor clean and dump all the dough onto flour-dusted plastic wrap and proceed.

Mixing Pie Dough by Hand

Mixing by hand is similar, but the resting and chilling period is even more important, allowing the flour to absorb all the moisture and avoiding puffy pockets of unincorporated flour in the dough. I like to use a box grater to create flakes of frozen butter when making dough by hand because—even though this method takes more time—the frozen butter doesn't lose structure and emulsify. Freeze the butter in sticks or blocks (not cubes) until solid. Weigh the flour into a large bowl. Using the largest holes on a box grater, shred the butter directly into the flour, intermittently fluffing the mixture so the butter doesn't clump. (If you don't have a box grater, cube the butter, chill it, and cut it into the flour with a pas-

try blender, two table knives, or by simply pinching it between your fingers.) Using your hands, quickly combine the ingredients until the ribbons of butter are lightly coated with flour. Work thoroughly and quickly. Pour in the cold liquid and use your hands to gather the ingredients. Rather than squeeze the dough, instead toss and fold, lightly pressing it into a sort of cohesive mass. It will take time for the flour to absorb the liquid, some of which happens while it rests, but work the mixture until all the flour is dampened and the dough is a shaggy clump. Scrape all the dough onto the flour-dusted plastic wrap and proceed.

Mixing Pie Dough with a Stand Mixer

This is a last resort dough-making option. It's the most challenging method because it is very difficult to control how rapidly the butter is cut in. Place the bowl of the stand mixer on the scale and weigh in the flour. Weigh in the very cold, but not frozen, cubed butter. The butter should give un-

Form a dough block.

Chill

der your fingertips but should not smush. Add the salt. Set the bowl on the mixer and use the paddle attachment on the lowest speed to gradually cut in the butter. This should take about 20 seconds. Pour in the cold liquid and combine on the lowest speed for less than 1 minute. Dump the dough, which will be very loose and barely contained, onto the flour-dusted plastic wrap and proceed.

FORMING THE DOUGH DISK OR BLOCK

Place two pieces of plastic wrap, each about 14 inches long, on the counter, crisscrossing them to form an X. Lightly dust the wrap's surface with flour. Scrape out the dough onto the center point of the X, loose and rough, and dust the top of the dough with a little more flour. Fold the plastic wrap over the dough, using it and a bench scraper—not your warm hands—to press it into shape.

If the dough will be used for a galette or a round tart, form it into a disk. If the dough will be rolled to a rectangle or a square, shape the dough into a block. The dough, when formed for chilling, should be about 1½ inches thick and either a 3- by 4-inch rectangular block, a 3½-inch square block, or a 4-inch diameter disk. The block or disk should be firm, compact, and without cracks and fissures. The more precise and compact this block is before chilling, the more straightforward it will be to roll out the dough to size, so be thoughtful and patient and use the leverage of the wrap to firm the sides and the sturdy blade of the bench scraper to square the edges. Tap the block or disk on the counter, rotating it around to get all the edges, then use the rolling pin to flatten the top and bottom. The dough will have precise edges, be studded with nubbins of butter, and wrapped snugly. Of course, you should also work quickly so the butter doesn't melt. This technique is a learned skill; each time you wrap the dough you will get better at it and soon it will be second nature.

CHILLING

Refrigerate the dough for at least 4 hours. During this time, any bit of slight overworking will be forgiven, the flour will absorb the liquid, and the butter and other fats will firm up. The cold fats, when introduced into a hot oven, will steam and puff, giving the crust loft and flake.

Or slip the wrapped dough into a ziptop bag and freeze it for up to 3 months. Defrost overnight in the refrigerator. Do not try to warm the dough in the microwave or on the counter. The dough will soften enough to roll in about 5 hours. I keep two or three pie doughs in the freezer at all times. If I'm making one dough recipe, I'll just roll up my sleeves and make four recipes consecutively. We love pie around here.

ROLLING

I want to assure you that rolling out pie dough is a skill that can be learned. No one is born with a rolling pin in their hand. With practice, making a pie and rolling out dough becomes a heavenly experience. A cold surface and a pin that feels good in the hand, with a weight that feels right, will help you find your rolling mojo. I have a drawer full of rolling pins: A long solid wooden cylinder that I use most often, a handled silicone pin that works perfectly when I am rolling large swaths of puff pastry, and a tapered wooden pin that I like for small dough projects like tiny tartlettes, fondant, or cookies. Find your favorite.

A Cold Surface

Ideally, after forming the plastic-wrapped dough into a block and a good long rest in the refrigerator, pie dough would be rolled out on a **cold stone counter.** I am fortunate. I have stone counters in

> ## DOUBLING DOUGH RECIPES
>
> Several recipes in this book call for two recipes of dough. I recommend making the batches consecutively, and not doubling the ingredients. It will be easier to roll out dough to the dimensions noted in the recipe, there is likely to be less dough waste, and the dough will come together more quickly, assuring a flakier pie. If you do decide to double the recipe, weigh the dough into equal portions before forming two dough disks or blocks. A double recipe of dough will require a large food processor, 11 cups or larger.

my kitchen, but during the summer months or when the oven has been on for a while, they are not cold enough. I remedy the situation by placing a sealed bag of ice on the counter for 10 minutes, then remove, dry the counter, and roll out the dough. That right there is the perfect situation.

We all know perfect situations are rare. So, if you have a small kitchen and not much counter real estate, try to establish enough space on another table or surface in your home or with **an (extra-large) piece of smooth marble, stone, or ceramic, or a wooden board** used especially for this purpose. Remnants or odd pieces can be found at stone yards and countertop companies.

Warm Slightly

As important as chilling the dough, bringing it to the correct temperature before rolling it out is equally crucial. Remove the dough from the refrigerator and let it warm slightly, no more than 10 minutes. Once a finger pressed into the surface makes a slight indentation without cracking, the dough is ready to roll. Do not let it get warmer or softer than this, and if it does, return it to the refrigerator for an hour before starting again. Rolling out dough that is too warm will smear the butter and other fats, resulting in no flake, a tough crust, and a sad pie maker. Rolling out dough that is too cold? That'll give you crumbling edges, cracks and tears, and more frustration. Give the dough time to slightly warm. Use the time to gather ingredients for the filling, turn on the oven, stir together the egg wash.

Get Prepared

To roll out the pie dough, prepare the rolling surface using blue painter's or masking tape to form a guide. The size will be specified in each recipe. Liberally dust the countertop with flour. Unwrap the dough, place it on the floured surface, and lightly flour the surface of the dough. Smack the block of dough three times with the rolling pin, flip the dough, and repeat on the other side. Smacking the dough is better at this point than rolling because it doesn't smear the fats, just compresses them. If the dough cracks when smacked, step back and allow additional time to warm, 2 or 3 minutes, then smack the dough again.

In a pinch, a wine bottle, a broom handle, or any cylindrical object will stand in for a rolling pin, making pie possible in any situation.

Dust with Flour and Roll

Begin to roll the dough from the center to the outside edges, away from you and toward you using firm, sure strokes, then vaguely to one side or the other, diagonally, guiding the shape. Sliding a bench scraper under any spots that stick, lift the dough and turn it a quarter turn and roll again. Check the size against the taped guide periodically. Dust with additional flour whenever the dough begins to stick to the pin or the counter. Do not press down with all your might and do not roll back and forth; instead, pick the pin up and roll up and pick the pin up and roll down, each time deftly pushing the dough until it is consistently thick and large enough to fit in the pan. Turn it 90 degrees to stretch and form the block to fit the taped size, moving it all the time to keep it from sticking. Try to avoid rolling over and flattening the edges of the dough.

If the dough bounces back and fights with you, don't fight back. Wait it out, just a couple of minutes, until the dough relaxes. Continually and lightly dust the pin, the dough, and the counter with flour, moving the dough around, using the bench scraper to lift the dough and roll it from another angle. Be quick and agile. Any cracks can be repaired, so don't worry. Don't obsess.

CHILLING, AGAIN

If possible, after rolling out the dough, chill it for 30 minutes or so to allow it to relax again and retain its layers. Then form the pastry into the shape and size called for in the recipe and chill again. Every pie and pie-like pastry in this book will benefit from a pre-bake chill. Fillings that are cold are easier to work with. Dough that is cold is easier to form. **When baking any flying pie, a pie without a pan, cold is essential to retaining the shape and reducing the spills.** At least 30 minutes in the freezer makes a world of difference. Custards do not freeze well, so instead, refrigerate any pastry with a filling that includes raw egg and milk.

BRUSHING WITH EGG WASH

Most of the pies in this book will be brushed with an egg wash before baking, which makes the pastry shiny and golden brown.

To make an egg wash, crack an egg into a small bowl. Add 1 tablespoon cool water and ¼ teaspoon salt. Salt helps break the egg down, encouraging the yolk and white to emulsify. Use a brush to lightly cover the top of the pastry with the wash, but do not paint the crimped edges. I like to use a silicone brush so no stray bristles are left behind.

BAKING

Pastry likes a hot oven. If you aren't getting the results you expect, evaluate your oven's temperature with an oven thermometer. A hot oven lets the butter bubble and burst, exposing beautiful layers of pastry. The back of the oven is hotter than the front, which is why baking sheets should be turned from front to back.

Hot on the Bottom

To avoid a soggy bottom crust, bake galettes, hand pies, empanadas, tarts, poppers, and all forms of pie dough on a hot surface. I like a Baking Steel (see Resources, page 275), baking stone, or inverted baking sheet that's been heating while the oven preheats. Placing the sheet pan holding a galette or a few hand pies atop this hot surface will brown the bottom crust, avoiding any sogginess.

STORING, FREEZING, AND REHEATING

Flying pies are the busy family's secret weapon. Most of the pastries in this book are great candidates for freezing. And many of the recipes make

ADJUSTING FOR ALTITUDE

- Baking at high altitudes means evaporation occurs more quickly and pie crusts and fillings tend to dry out. To avoid a desiccated pie:

- Increase the oven temperature by 15°F at 3,000 feet; 20°F at 5,000 feet; and 25°F at 7,500 feet.

- For all crusts, increase the flour by 1 tablespoon at 3,000 feet, and an additional 1 tablespoon for every 1,000 feet over 3,000. (Example: If baking at 6,000 feet, add 4 tablespoons flour to the crust recipe.)

- Decrease sugar in the filling by 1 tablespoon over 3,000 feet.

- Increase liquid in the filling by 2 tablespoons at 3,000 feet and 4 tablespoons at 7,500 feet.

- Visual cues are always a better indication of doneness. For a rule of thumb, expect to decrease the baking time by around 5 minutes at 3,000 feet and 8 minutes at 7,500 feet.

enough to warrant popping something in the freezer, squirreled away for another day. They're lunch, after-school snacks, and supper, alongside a bowl of soup.

Freeze flying pies either unbaked or already baked. Place the pies apart on a parchment-lined baking sheet and freeze solid. Slip into a ziptop bag, label, and freeze for up to 3 months.

Pies with custards or pastry cream cannot be frozen and should be kept refrigerated until serving. Fruit pies and nut pies may be safely stored overnight on the counter, tightly covered, but anything containing meat, fish, chicken, eggs, or dairy should be refrigerated.

The freezer is incredibly useful for all aspects of pie making. Keep pie dough at the ready. It holds in the refrigerator for 2 days and in the freezer for 3 months. Frozen pie dough will defrost in about 5 hours in the refrigerator. Dream up a galette at breakfast, make it and bake it after work.

When making pie dough, I'll make two, or four, and freeze blocks of dough for future oppor-tunities. When I am in the kitchen making pie and there's flour on the counter already, I might make a few hand pies or pie poppers, too. Freeze them, either baked or unbaked, and a dinner or dessert will be just 30 minutes away.

To reheat almost any of the pies in this book, place on a parchment-lined baking sheet, and bake at 350°F for about 15 minutes. Plunge a knife into the center then touch the tip of the knife to see if the filling is hot. If not, continue to warm the pie for another 5 to 10 minutes.

Hand pies, pie poppers, knishes, kolache, empanadas—all of these flying pies will reheat in a toaster oven, so they're kid-friendly after-school-hunger-busters, too.

ALL-BUTTER PIE DOUGH

Makes 1 recipe pie dough

1⅓ cups (160 g) all-purpose flour

8 tablespoons (113 g) unsalted butter, cubed and frozen for 20 minutes

Scant pinch kosher salt

¼ cup (60 ml) ice water

Be a fearless pie baker with this dependably delicious, absolutely consistent pie dough. It is my hands-down favorite crust. It is easy to handle, freezes beautifully, and crimps like a dream. This crust fits the bill whether baking up a sweet or savory galette, hand pie, or popper. (See page 244 to make the dough by hand or in a stand mixer.)

Place the work bowl of the food processor on the scale, set the scale to zero, and weigh the flour into the bowl. Weigh in the butter and add the salt. Move the bowl to the food processor base, insert the metal blade, cover, and use the Pulse function to cut the flour and butter into flour-covered pea-sized pieces, about 15 quick pulses. Add the ice water all at once and process until the dough almost comes together in a ball. All the flour will be dampened and the dough will clump.

Spend time on this next step because the more compact and precise the dough, the easier it is to roll to the correct size and thickness. Form an X with two long pieces of overlapping plastic wrap and lightly flour the surface. Dump the dough onto the center of the plastic wrap, scraping the processor bowl clean. Wrap the sloppy gathering of dough in the plastic and, at the same time, use a bench scraper (not your warm hands that might melt the butter clumps) to form the dough into a 4-inch disk or a 3½- by 3½-inch block. Once wrapped, use a rolling pin to gently press across the surface of the dough, then flip it over and do the same on the other side. Now let it rest: Refrigerate the dough for at least 4 hours or preferably overnight. Alternatively, slip the plastic-wrapped dough block into a ziptop bag and freeze it for up to 3 months. Defrost gently, overnight in the refrigerator.

CREAM CHEESE PIE DOUGH

Makes 1 recipe pie dough

1⅓ cups (160 g) all-purpose flour

4 tablespoons (56 g) unsalted butter, cubed and frozen for 20 minutes

4 tablespoons (2 ounces, 56 g) cream cheese, cubed and refrigerated for 20 minutes

⅛ teaspoon kosher salt

¼ cup (60 ml) ice water

This tender, slightly tangy crust snuggles up to both sweet and savory fillings. It's sturdy enough to cut into shapes, loves a good crimp, stands tall on the sides, and shines under an egg wash. Use full-fat cream cheese in a block, not whipped. (See page 244 to make the dough by hand or in a stand mixer.)

Place the work bowl of the food processor on the scale, set the scale to zero, and weigh the flour into the bowl. Weigh in the butter and cream cheese and add the salt. Move the bowl to the food processor base, insert the metal blade, cover, and use the Pulse function to cut the flour, butter, and cream cheese into flour-covered pea-sized pieces, about 15 quick pulses. Add the ice water all at once and process until the dough almost comes together in a ball. All the flour will be dampened and the dough will clump.

Spend time on this next step because the more compact and precise the dough, the easier it is to roll to the correct size and thickness. Form an X with two long pieces of over-lapping plastic wrap and lightly flour the surface. Dump the dough onto the center of the plastic wrap, scraping the processor bowl clean. Wrap the sloppy gathering of dough in plastic and, at the same time, use a bench scraper (not your warm hands that might melt the fat clumps) to form the dough into a 4-inch disk or a 3½- by 3½-inch block. Once wrapped, use a rolling pin to gently press across the surface of the dough, then flip it over and do the same on the other side. Now let it rest: Refrigerate the dough for at least 4 hours or preferably overnight. Alternatively, slip the plastic-wrapped dough block into a ziptop bag and freeze it for up to 3 months. Defrost gently, overnight in the refrig-erator.

SHORTENING PIE DOUGH

Makes 1 recipe pie dough

1⅓ cups (160 g) all-purpose flour

4 tablespoons (56 g) unsalted butter, cubed and frozen for 20 minutes

4 tablespoons (56 g) Spectrum or other vegetable shortening, cubed and frozen for 20 minutes

⅛ teaspoon kosher salt

¼ cup (60 ml) ice water

1 tablespoon vodka (optional)

Shortening is the vegetarian version of lard and a pie maker's friend for flaky yet sturdy, tender yet sandy, bronzed yet crisp pie crust. A shortening crust will have a longer life, staying flaky and crisp for an extra day or two more than an all-butter crust. Include at least half butter for flavor. This is a sturdy dough, easy to roll, patch, crimp, and decorate. (See page 244 to make the dough by hand or in a stand mixer.)

Place the work bowl of the food processor on the scale, set the scale to zero, and weigh the flour into the bowl. Weigh in the butter and shortening and add the salt. Move the bowl to the food processor base, insert the metal blade, cover, and use the Pulse function to cut the flour, butter, and shortening into flour-covered pea-sized pieces, about 15 quick pulses. Add the ice water and vodka (if using) all at once and process until the dough almost comes together in a ball. All the flour will be dampened and the dough will clump.

Spend time on this next step because the more compact and precise the dough, the easier it is to roll to the correct size and thickness. Form an X with two long pieces of overlapping plastic wrap and lightly flour the surface. Dump the dough onto the center of the plastic wrap, scraping the processor bowl clean. Wrap the sloppy gathering of dough in plastic and, at the same time, use a bench scraper (not your warm hands that might melt the fat clumps) to form the dough into a 4-inch disk or a 3½- by 3½-inch block. Once wrapped, use a rolling pin to gently press across the surface of the dough, then flip it over and do the same on the other side. Now let it rest: Refrigerate the dough for at least 4 hours or preferably overnight. Alternatively, slip the plastic-wrapped dough block into a ziptop bag and freeze it for up to 3 months. Defrost gently, overnight in the refrigerator.

BROWN-BUTTER PIE DOUGH

Makes 1 recipe pie dough

8 tablespoons
(113 g) unsalted
butter

1½ cups (160 g)
all-purpose flour

⅛ teaspoon
kosher salt

¼ cup (60 ml)
ice cold water

Browned butter adds a nutty flavor and a caramel note to a baked crust. It's worth the extra steps, especially in the most elegant fruit tarts. (See page 244 to make the dough by hand or in a stand mixer.)

In a medium saucepan over medium-high heat, melt the butter until it begins to sizzle and pop. Small browned bits will drop to the bottom of the pan and the room will be filled with a buttery, nutty scent. Stay alert. This is the moment when everything can go topsy-turvy. Once the butter stops spitting and popping, going dead silent (a great tip from Stella Parks of BraveTart), and gets pretty brown, pour it into a glass or metal bowl, leaving the dark bits on the bottom of the pan. Chill this browned butter until hard, about 2 hours at least, and then cube and proceed with the recipe. (To speed cleanup, fill the saucepan with water and bring it to a boil to dislodge those pesky dark bits sticking to the bottom of the pan.)

Place the work bowl of the food processor on the scale, set the scale to zero, and weigh the flour into the bowl. Add in the butter and salt. Move the bowl to the food processor base, insert the metal blade, cover, and use the Pulse function to cut the flour and butter into flour-covered pea-sized pieces, about 15 quick pulses. Add the cold water all at once and process until the dough almost comes together in a ball. All the flour will be dampened and the dough will clump.

Spend time on this next step because the more compact and precise the dough, the easier it is to roll to the correct size and thickness. Form an X with two long pieces of overlapping plastic wrap and lightly flour the surface. Dump the dough onto the center of the plastic wrap, scraping the processor bowl clean. Wrap the sloppy gathering of dough in plastic and, at the same time, use a bench scraper (not your warm hands that might melt the butter clumps) to form the dough into a 4-inch disk or a 3½- by 3½-inch block. Once wrapped, use a rolling pin to gently press across the surface of the dough, then flip it over and do the same on the other side. Now let it rest: Refrigerate the dough for at least 4 hours or preferably overnight. Alternatively, slip the plastic-wrapped dough block into a ziptop bag and freeze for up to 3 months. Defrost gently, overnight in the refrigerator.

CHOCOLATE PIE DOUGH

Makes 1 recipe pie dough

1⅓ cups (165 g) all-purpose flour

Scant 3 tablespoons (18 g) natural (not Dutched) cocoa powder

Generous 3 tablespoons (40 g) granulated sugar

8 tablespoons (113 g) unsalted butter, diced and frozen for 20 minutes

⅛ teaspoon kosher salt

¼ cup (60 ml) coffee, ice cold

Powdered sugar for dusting and rolling the dough

Chocolate pie dough is notoriously challenging to work with, but it is such a lovely merging of pie dough and shortbread, with a glorious crackly texture, that the effort is well spent. This is not a sweet dough, but it's a terrific foil for sweet fillings. Use powdered sugar to dust the counter, never flour; adding flour will make this already strong dough tough. (See page 244 to make the dough by hand or in a stand mixer.)

Place the work bowl of the food processor on the scale, set the scale to zero, and weigh the flour into the bowl. Weigh in the cocoa, then the granulated sugar and the butter; add the salt. Move the bowl to the food processor base, insert the metal blade, cover, and use the Pulse function to cut the mixture into flour-covered pea-sized pieces, about 15 quick pulses. Add the coffee all at once and process until the dough almost comes together in a ball. All the dry ingredients will be dampened and the dough will clump.

Spend time on this next step because the more compact and precise the dough, the easier it is to roll to the correct size and thickness. Form an X with two long pieces of overlapping plastic wrap and lightly dust the surface with powdered sugar. Dump the dough onto the center of the plastic wrap, scraping the processor bowl clean. Wrap the sloppy gathering of dough in plastic and, at the same time, use a bench scraper (not your warm hands that might melt the butter clumps) to form the dough into a 4-inch disk or a 3½- by 3½-inch block. Once wrapped, use a rolling pin to gently press across the surface of the dough, then flip it over and do the same on the other side. Now let it rest: Refrigerate the dough for at least 4 hours or preferably overnight. Alternatively, slip the plastic-wrapped dough block into a ziptop bag and freeze it for up to 3 months. Defrost gently, overnight in the refrigerator.

EVERYTHING SPICE PIE DOUGH

Makes 1 recipe pie dough

1⅓ cups (160 g) all-purpose flour

8 tablespoons (113 g) unsalted butter, cubed and frozen for 20 minutes

1 tablespoon Everything Spice Mix (recipe follows)

⅛ teaspoon kosher salt

¼ cup (60 ml) ice water

'm a fool for an everything bagel, and while dreaming up crust combinations for this book, it seemed an obvious choice to put a little spice in the pie dough. The seeds, garlic, onion, and salt contribute a marvelous textural and flavorful nuance to meaty hand pies and galettes. (See page 244 to make the dough by hand or in a stand mixer.)

Place the work bowl of the food processor on the scale, set the scale to zero, and weigh the flour into the bowl. Weigh in the butter and add the spice mix and salt. Move the bowl to the food processor base, insert the metal blade, cover, and use the Pulse function to cut the flour and butter into flour-covered pea-sized pieces, about 15 quick pulses. Add the ice water all at once and process until the dough almost comes together in a ball. All the flour will be dampened and the dough will clump.

Spend time on this next step because the more compact and precise the dough, the easier it is to roll to the correct size and thickness. Form an X with two long pieces of overlapping plastic wrap and lightly flour the surface. Dump the dough onto the center of the plastic wrap, scraping the processor bowl clean. Wrap the sloppy gathering of dough in plastic and, at the same time, use a bench scraper (not your warm hands that might melt the butter clumps) to form the dough into a 4-inch disk or a 3½- by 3½-inch block. Once wrapped, use a rolling pin to gently press across the surface of the dough, then flip it over and do the same on the other side. Now let it rest: Refrigerate the dough for at least 4 hours or preferably overnight. Alternatively, slip the plastic-wrapped dough block into a ziptop bag and freeze it for up to 3 months. Defrost gently, overnight in the refrigerator.

EVERYTHING SPICE MIX

Makes about ¼ cup

2 tablespoons
poppy seeds

2 tablespoons
toasted sesame
seeds

1 tablespoon dried
minced onion

2 teaspoons dried
minced garlic

2 teaspoons
Maldon salt or
coarse *fleur de sel*

It's called Everything Spice for a reason. Put in there what you like. The recipe below is my basic combination, but sometimes I'll add fennel seeds or crushed red pepper. Other times, I leave out the garlic and add charnushka (nigella) seeds. Make your own everything mix and make it all yours. Asian markets sell large canisters of already toasted sesame seeds. Keep them refrigerated and they'll be close at hand and find their way into so many things. Sniff poppy seeds to make sure they haven't turned rancid; it happens very quickly.

In a small jar, mix the poppy seeds, sesame seeds, onion, garlic, and salt. Cover and store in the refrigerator.

CARAMELIZED ONION AND CHEESE PIE DOUGH

Makes 1 recipe pie dough

---

2 ounces (56 g) extra sharp cheddar cheese (preferably orange), cold

1⅓ cups (160 g) all-purpose flour

1 recipe Onion Butter (recipe follows), cubed and chilled

¼ teaspoon kosher salt

¼ cup (60 ml) ice water

Plan some time to make this dough as the onion butter needs to chill hard. It's a super savory flavor to wrap around almost any meaty filling. Flour the board and rolling pin generously; this is a sticky dough and it warms quickly. The dough will bake more quickly than all-butter and shortening doughs, so if you choose to swap it into another recipe, keep your eye on the oven and watch for visual cues like over-browning, and tent with foil, if needed. (See page 244 to make the dough by hand or in a stand mixer.)

Roughly chop the cheese into pea-sized pieces, about ½ cup packed.

Place the work bowl of the food processor on the scale, set the scale to zero, and weigh the flour into the bowl. Weigh in the onion butter and cheese. Finally, add the salt. Move the bowl to the food processor base, insert the metal blade, cover, and use the Pulse function to cut the flour, butter, and cheese into flour-covered pea-sized pieces, about 15 quick pulses. Add the ice water all at once and process until the dough almost comes together in a ball. All the flour will be dampened and the dough will clump.

Spend time on this next step because the more compact and precise the dough, the easier it is to roll to the correct size and thickness. Form an X with two long pieces of overlapping plastic wrap and lightly flour the surface. Dump the dough onto the center of the plastic wrap, scraping the processor bowl clean. Wrap the sloppy gathering of dough in the plastic and, at the same time, use a bench scraper (not your warm hands that might melt the butter clumps) to form the dough into a 4-inch disk or a 3½- by 3½-inch block.

Once wrapped, use a rolling pin to gently press across the surface of the dough, then flip it over and do the same on the other side. Now let it rest: Refrigerate the dough for at least 4 hours or preferably overnight. Alternatively, slip the plastic-wrapped dough block into a ziptop bag and freeze it for up to 3 months. Defrost gently, overnight in the refrigerator.

ONION BUTTER (COMPOUND BUTTER)

Makes enough for 1 recipe pie dough

8 tablespoons (113 g) unsalted butter, at room temperature

½ cup (70 g) diced onion (about 1 small)

Compound butter (a fancy name for flavored butter) is a wildly useful secret weapon for any cook. It refers to butter infused with a flavor, like lemon or garlic or, in this case, slowly caramelized onions. Chop the onions very finely so they disperse throughout the butter. Double the recipe so you have onion butter to plop on a steak just as it comes off the grill.

Cube the butter into ½-inch pieces and place in a large mixing bowl. Take out a good-sized portion of butter from the bowl, about 2 tablespoons, and heat until bubbling in a small skillet over low heat. Add the onions to the melted butter, stir well, and cook over low heat for 20 to 25 minutes, stirring lazily from time to time. The onions should be soft, browned, and smelling nice and sweet. Let cool for a few minutes.

Scrape the onions, melted butter, and all the delicious brown bits into the bowl with the butter cubes. Knead the onions into the butter with your fingers or a rubber spatula. Wrap the butter in plastic wrap, then form it into a block. Refrigerate until very cold, at least 2 hours. Cube the onion butter and chill until ready to make the crust.

THE PASTRY DOUGHS

Pulled, layered, rolled, fried, and boosted with yeast and baking powder, these pie-adjacent doughs deserve a place in the fleet of flying pies. They are worthy wrappings for any filling. Cross-cultural, leftover-extending meals are ready-made with these reliable doughs.

PULLED DOUGH FOR STRUDEL

Makes 1 strudel sheet, about 20 by 24 inches when pulled

1¼ cups (150 g)
all-purpose flour

¼ teaspoon
kosher salt

3 tablespoons
grapeseed or
canola oil

⅓ cup (80 ml)
cool water

Strudel dough is not rolled out with a pin, but stretched. (See page 138 for the technique and pages 142 to 151 for the strudel recipes.) Because of this, the dough needs to be very elastic, requiring well-developed gluten, which means active, extensive kneading. Kneading can be tiresome, so do as generations of Germans, Austrians, and Alsatians have done, and slap the dough on the counter with vigor instead. Just lift it up and slap it down, turn, fold, and do it again. And again. In fact, most classic strudel dough recipes include the direction to lift and slap the dough on the counter 100 or more times. It's a great way to get out that daily *grr*, and a good workout for the arms. But if you aren't feeling the slapping, you can knead in the usual way, folding and pushing the dough away from you, and then turning it 90 degrees and continuing the fold and push and turn action for 10 minutes. Alternatively, put the organized dough ball in the stand mixer with the dough hook, and let the machine do the work for 10 full minutes. I like the dough slapping; it feels more authentic.

In a wide bowl, using a table fork, stir together the flour and salt. Make a well in the center and pour in the oil. Gather the flour into the oil with the fork. Pour in the water slowly, continuing to use the fork to incorporate the flour, until the dough is shaggy and wet. It will look impossible and you will be unhappy with me, but please persist.

Let go of the fork, lightly flour your hands, and work inside the bowl to gather the dough (which, admittedly, is more like batter). Just lift and turn, fold and lift, and unbelievably the dough will begin to feel silky and smooth and come together after 5 minutes or so. It's a miracle.

Move the dough ball onto a very lightly floured counter and knead for 10 minutes; or slap it vigorously 100 times (see headnote); or place the dough ball in the stand mixer and, with the dough hook in place, let the mixer knead the dough for 10 minutes.

Lightly coat the inside of a ziptop bag with cooking spray and place the dough in the bag. After a 30-minute rest on the counter, seal the bag and refrigerate overnight before stretching the dough.

Strudel dough can be refrigerated for up to 2 days and cannot be successfully frozen.

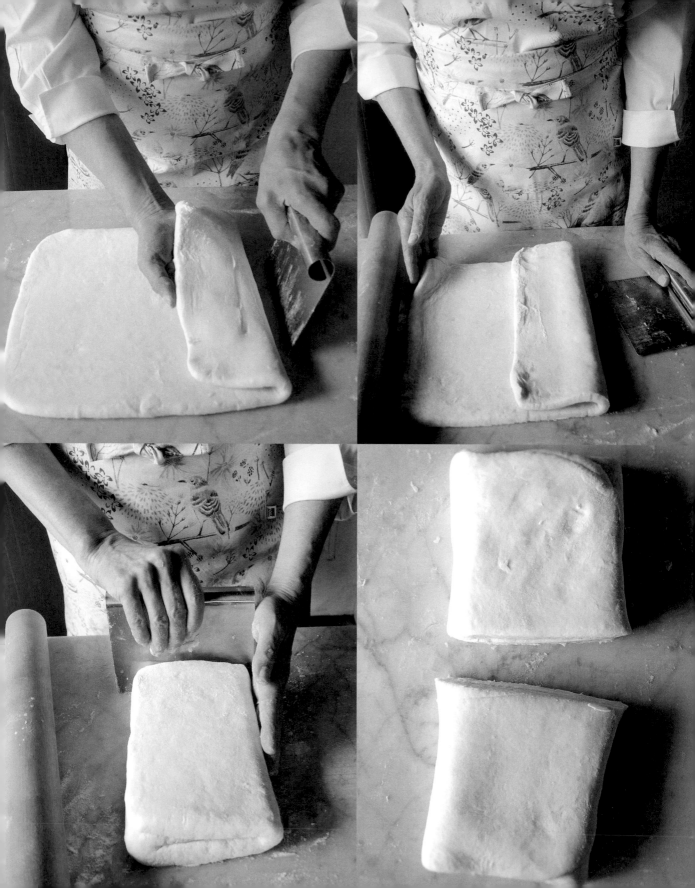

QUICK PUFF PASTRY

Makes 1 block (20 ounces, 500 g)

2 cups (240 g)
all-purpose flour

¾ teaspoon
kosher salt

16 tablespoons
(226 g) unsalted
butter, cut into
½-inch dice and
refrigerated at
least 1 hour

½ cup (120 ml)
cold water

¼ teaspoon
freshly squeezed
lemon juice

Puff pastry is laminated dough, a reference to the layers folded into a buttery mass. Traditional puff pastry uses nothing but flour and butter, the butter beaten flat and then folded and rolled and folded and rolled and reworked four times, each called a "turn." Here, in the quick version of traditional puff, the dough is made in the mixer, the folds and turns happen all at once, and it's much less work. (If this seems difficult, it's worth making real puff pastry once to see what a joy this version is.) I like to make a double recipe, and then cut it into two portions, freezing one for later.

I make puff with regular American-style butter because that's what is usually in my freezer, but you can use lovely fancy butter if you wish. This pastry is all about buttery flake and flavor. In the recipes on pages 157 to 163, you'll be most successful rolling and portioning if you remain obsessively diligent about keeping the dough very very cold, never never never smeary, and the edges of the dough block and the rolled dough very squared and even. Use the bench scraper to make those crisp edges. Be obsessive.

Place the flour and salt in the bowl of a stand mixer with the paddle attachment. With the mixer on low, add the butter a few cubes at a time until the dough is a collection of little bits about the size of jelly beans. It should seem dry-ish and pebbly. With the mixer still running, add the water and lemon juice in a steady stream. Mix for 30 seconds. Turn out the crumbly dough onto the work surface and, using your hands and a bench scraper, press and shape the dough into a long firm rectangle 10 by 5 inches.

Use the bench scraper to fold the dough in thirds, like a business letter, so it is about 5 by 3 inches. Turn the dough

(Continued)

OPPOSITE:
Quick Puff Pastry techniques (doubled recipe)

90 degrees and reroll the dough into a rectangle 10 by 5 inches. Repeat the folding and rotating three times for a total of four turns. If the dough becomes too sticky to work with, place it on a baking sheet and chill until firm, then resume your rolling and turning.

Form an X with two long pieces of overlapping plastic wrap and lightly flour the surface. Place the tidy rectangle in the center of the plastic wrap. Wrap the dough in the plastic and, at the same time, use a bench scraper to form the squared sides of the 5- by 3-inch block. Once wrapped, use a rolling pin to gently press across the surface of the block, smoothing the top. Flip it over and do the same on the other side. Square it up again. Now let it rest: Refrigerate the dough for at least 4 hours or preferably overnight. Quick Puff Pastry will keep refrigerated for 3 days or in a ziptop bag in the freezer for 3 months. Defrost in the refrigerator overnight.

BUTTERMILK DOUGH FOR FRIED FRUIT PIES

Makes enough dough for 12 (3-inch) fried pies

---

3 cups (360 g)
all-purpose flour

½ cup (113 g)
lard or vegetable
shortening, at
room temperature

3 tablespoons
granulated sugar

½ teaspoon
kosher salt

1 cup (240 ml)
buttermilk, at
room temperature

With an exterior that tastes like the best carnival funnel cake, the fried pies on pages 199 to 209 have a shattering dough that blisters on the surface. Buttermilk provides tang, acidity, and lift and it's appropriately reverential to great Southern cuisine, where buttermilk is king. The dough is damp but pulls together as it chills.

Place the work bowl of the food processor on the scale, set the scale to zero, and weigh the flour into the bowl. Weigh in the shortening and then add the sugar and salt. Move the bowl to the food processor base, insert the metal blade, cover, and use the Pulse function to cut the flour and shortening into flour-covered pea-sized pieces, about 15 quick pulses. Add the buttermilk all at once, then process until the dough almost comes together in a ball, wet and batter-like.

Generously flour the counter and scrape the dough out of the bowl. Turn the dough over to coat in flour, then gather the loose mass, fold it over on itself a couple of times, and form a soft block about 6 by 4 inches. Form an X with two long pieces of overlapping plastic wrap and lightly flour the surface. Dump the dough onto the center of the plastic wrap. Wrap the dough in the plastic and, at the same time, use a bench scraper (not your warm hands that might melt the shortening clumps) to form the dough.

Once wrapped, use a rolling pin to gently press across the surface of the block. Flip it over and do the same on the other side. Now let it rest: Refrigerate the dough for at least 4 hours or preferably overnight. Alternatively, slip the plastic-wrapped dough block into a ziptop bag and freeze for up to 3 months. Defrost gently, overnight in the refrigerator.

EMPANADA DOUGH THAT'S FIT TO BE FRIED

Makes enough dough for 18 (5-inch) fried empanadas

3 cups (360 g)
all-purpose flour

1 tablespoon
granulated sugar

1½ teaspoons
kosher salt

1 teaspoon
baking powder

⅓ cup (68 g)
shortening or lard,
cubed and chilled

1 cup (240 ml)
whole milk, cold

This dough for the Oozy Cheese Fried Empanadas (page 187) has a touch of baking powder for lift, along with shortening, or (my preference) lard, to make big beautiful bubbles on the exterior of these fried treats.

Place the work bowl of the food processor on the scale, set the scale to zero, and weigh the flour into the bowl. Add the sugar, salt, and baking powder, stir, and weigh in the shortening. Move the bowl to the food processor base, insert the metal blade, cover, and use the Pulse function to cut the flour and shortening into flour-covered pea-sized pieces, about 15 quick pulses. Add the cold milk all at once and process until the dough almost comes together in a ball. All the flour will be dampened and the dough will clump.

Spend time on this next step because the more compact and precise the dough, the easier it is to roll to the correct size and thickness. Form an X with two long pieces of overlapping plastic wrap and lightly flour the surface. Dump the dough onto the center of the plastic wrap, scraping the processor bowl clean. Wrap the sloppy gathering of dough in plastic and, at the same time, use a bench scraper (not your warm hands that might melt the fat clumps) to form the squared sides of a block about 6 by 4 inches. Once wrapped, use a rolling pin to gently press across the surface of the block. Flip it over and do the same on the other side. Now let it rest: Refrigerate the dough for at least 1 hour.

This dough does not freeze well but may be made in advance and refrigerated for up to 2 days.

ENRICHED YEAST DOUGH FOR KOLACHE

Makes enough dough for 12 kolache

2¼ teaspoons active dry yeast (one packet)

1¼ cups (300 ml) lukewarm water

¼ cup (50 g) granulated sugar

5 cups (600 g) all-purpose flour, plus extra for kneading and forming

2 large eggs

4 tablespoons (56 g) unsalted butter, cubed

1 teaspoon kosher salt

A classic Eastern and Northern European sweet dough, this is the one I like for kolache (pages 213 to 226). In the Old Country, every sort of baked treat is made with this bouncy, airy, lovely dough. I've seen cookies made with the dough, and jam-filled pastries formed like a Danish, and even pizza-style round tarts covered with jam. But I love the buns—kolache—stuffed with either sweet or savory filling. If I know I'll be making only sweet buns, I might add up to a teaspoon of citrus zest or cinnamon, or ½ teaspoon ground cardamom to the dough. If savory, I might add ½ teaspoon smoked paprika or sumac, or a pinch of cayenne. When the dough isn't flavored, of course, it's possible to make one batch of dough and two or three different filled kolache. Don't let the yeast part scare you. This is a happy dough—easy to pull together in the stand mixer. It feels great under the hand and the rolling pin.

In the bottom of the stand mixer's bowl, bloom the yeast by scattering it over ¼ cup of the warm water. If it does not foam enthusiastically in a few minutes, discard and replace the yeast before continuing. Add the sugar to the yeast mixture and stir together. Add the remaining 1 cup water, the flour, eggs, butter, and salt. Using the dough hook with the mixer set at "4," or medium, beat and knead the mixture for 7 to 10 minutes, stopping once or twice to scrape the bowl, until strands are forming on the sides of the bowl and the dough is smooth with tiny bubbles dotting the surface. It will be sticky and will not form a ball but will be starting to pull away from the sides of the bowl. Do not hesitate to add up to 3 tablespoons additional flour if the dough is not coming together. This is a dough that is dry on a dry day and wet on a wet day, so on a rainy day, you may need more flour.

Use cooking spray to lightly oil a large bowl. Dust the work surface with flour. Scrape the dough onto the work surface and lightly flour the surface of the dough. Using a bench scraper, lift and fold the dough, turning, lifting and folding again a few times, until it moves freely. Place in the prepared bowl and cover with plastic wrap. Settle the bowl in a warm, draft-free place and let the dough rise until doubled in size, about 1 hour. For a long, slow rise, refrigerate the dough for up to 16 hours and bring to room temperature for an hour before proceeding with making the kolache. (see Making Kolache, page 214).

DAIRY-FREE DOUGH FOR KNISHES

Makes enough dough for 18 knishes

½ cup (120 ml) neutral oil (like grapeseed) or schmaltz (rendered chicken, duck, or goose fat)

¼ to ⅓ cup (60 to 80 ml) cool water

1 large egg

1 teaspoon white vinegar

½ teaspoon kosher salt

2½ cups (300 g) all-purpose flour

1 teaspoon baking powder

This is an oily dough and feels all wrong when you start making it. You will question me and my recipe, but let it rest for an hour before you take any rash action. Once you start making the knishes, pages 232 to 239, a dough emerges that's silky, easy to roll and stretch, and a breeze to shape. You mustn't refrigerate or freeze knish dough; it becomes too stiff and impossible to wrestle into shape.

Whisk the oil, ¼ cup water, egg, vinegar, and salt in a small bowl. In a large bowl, whisk the flour and baking powder. Make a well in the center of the dry ingredients and pour in the wet ingredients, mixing with a table fork to incorporate. If the mixture seems dry, add the remaining water and continue mixing. Turn the dough out and knead until silky, smooth, and elastic, about 8 minutes. Place the dough ball back in the large bowl, cover, and let it rest for 1 hour.

THE GROCERY STORE SHORTCUTS

The grocery store holds excellent options that serve the same function as any dough for flying pies—something in which we can easily nestle a filling, making the most of something delicious.

Of course, there are **pie doughs** available in the freezer section, but I'm not a fan. There, I've said it. If you must, look for those with good ingredients like butter and no ingredient you can't pronounce or find in your own pantry. A storebought 9- or 10-inch crust will substitute for a single recipe of my pie crusts, and will form a galette or tart readily. When cutting out circles for hand pies or poppers or empanadas, grocery store dough may not yield the same number of pieces.

I may make my own **puff pastry** (page 265), but I also buy it. Dufour is my favorite brand as it's made with all butter. Trader Joe's also carries an all-butter version, but not in all stores and not all the time. Grocery store puff sheets are not as generously sized as homemade, but they can be substituted into the recipes using puff pastry (pages 157 to 163). Look for the largest puff sheets available—the recipes call for the dough to be rolled to a 10- by 16-inch and a 12- by 12-inch form. Technique tips for puff pastry are on page 156. The recipes are on pages 157 to 163.

Phyllo sheets are readily available in the grocery store's frozen section. I keep a box of phyllo in the freezer all the time, just in case. One supermarket box will make any of the recipes, with some leftover. Technique tips for phyllo are on page 168. The recipes are on pages 171 to 173.

Spring roll wrappers are made for frying, so any kind of filling may be tucked into a wrapper; the technique is shown on page 196, and the recipes are on pages 199 to 204. Never overfill the wrapper, they're very thin and delicate and they will burst. The wrappers may be frozen and defrosted overnight in the refrigerator before using. Rice paper wrappers are not the same thing.

RESOURCES

EQUIPMENT

Baking sheets, in quarter- and half-sheet sizes (9 by 13 inches or 13 by 18 inches) are indispensable in the kitchen. I must have six or eight of each size. While flying pies require no pie-specific pans, they do all need to bake on a baking sheet. I place my ingredients on a baking sheet to organize them (mis en place). I reheat last night's pie on one. I toast nuts on another. They are widely available at places like Sur La Table, Target, Walmart, hardware stores, and any restaurant supply store, as well as online. I have two or three that came with a snap-on plastic cover, and another one or two that came with racks inside, so look for values!

A Baking Steel, my secret weapon for fighting a soggy bottom, is available from www.bakingsteel.com. I have a 16- by 14-inch version, weighing in at about 15 pounds. If you make bread or pizza, you will be so happy to have this addition to your kitchen arsenal.

Using a **digital kitchen scale** will help you make pies that are consistently delicious. I'm fond of the OXO scale because it offers a flat base on which to place the food processor bowl and the numbers are back-lit and large enough to read easily. You'll find this and other digital scales available online, and at Target, Walmart, Bed Bath & Beyond, Sur La Table, and Williams Sonoma. I promise you will see results in your baking as well as fewer dishes to wash!

I don't use my **food processor** all the time, but I do use it every time for pastry. Nothing cuts in butter faster and more consistently than the food processor. I've used an 11-cup model from Cuisinart for years. It's a dependable kitchen workhorse and worth the investment. Food processors can be found at all department stores' kitchen departments, Sur La Table, Williams Sonoma, Bed Bath & Beyond, Target, Walmart, and Costco, and online. A big motor and a big work bowl are nice to have. Replacement work bowls, lids, and blades are available from the manufacturer or from websites like kitchenworksinc.com.

I resisted the call of the **Vitamix heavy-duty blender** for a while, but I'm very glad I gave in. It's a useful machine, sturdy and strong. Available at Sur La Table, Target, Walmart, Costco, and online. I use the Vitamix to pulverize bread crumbs, nuts, and Parmigiano, to make the silkiest squash and apple soup, to make sauces, juices, and so much more.

Silicone brushes, bench scrapers, cookie cutters, pastry dockers, and fluted pastry wheels are available at kitchenware shops like Sur La Table, Bed Bath & Beyond, Williams Sonoma, and Target. Online sites like kitchenkrafts.com carry many items useful for pie-making. And I love to find vintage tools when I'm out poking around yard sales.

When I learned that I could buy **parchment sheets** pre-cut to fit baking sheets, my kitchen life improved. I buy 100 sheets at a time and I couldn't be happier to have that stack of pristine white sheets ready when I need them, no cutting required. You'll find parchment and more baking essentials at kingarthurflour.com.

Finding your **rolling pin,** the one that fits your hand, may take some time. Be deliberate. Borrow your friend's. Use your mom's. Figure out what shape and weight works best. The helpful staff at Williams Sonoma or Sur La Table can help sort the wood from the silicone, the handled from the cylindrical from the tapered.

Cherry pitters are very nice to have. When faced with two flats of cherries, I appreciated the type with a hopper, but for a few quarts at a time, I am partial to the handheld version from OXO.

INGREDIENTS

I've used King Arthur flour to develop these recipes. Their all purpose flour is available in many grocery stores, at Target, some Walmarts and Costcos, and online directly from the Vermont headquarters, kingarthurflour.com.

For decorating, **sparkling and pearl sugars, white and multicolored and chocolate jimmies and sprinkles** can be found in most grocery store baking aisles. Larger containers (which are more affordable, ounce for ounce) are available at Sur La Table, Michaels, Bed Bath & Beyond, and online. Fancy decorating baubles from Sweetapolita (Sweetapolita.com) are special-occasion beautiful, a little spendy, but worth it.

The recipes in this book use Diamond Crystal **kosher salt.** I find it at my grocery store, restaurant supply stores, and Costco. If using Morton's kosher salt, cut back just a little as it's heavier by weight.

Nuts and dried fruit from Nuts.com are so delicious and fresh, especially true of their dried strawberries, I'm converted to ordering online. When I don't have the time to order, I think the fruits and nuts at Trader Joe's are superior. They're fresh and packaged in reasonably sized containers.

Jarred spices purchased at the grocery store can be old and dusty. I order **spices, chile peppers, salts, and vanilla** from Penzeys (penzeys.com).

Meyer lemons are a weakness of mine. These hybrid lemons are sweet and juicy and wonderful and so pretty, I always fill a bowl with them just to look at their cheery yellow. Available more widely now than they were years ago, tucked into the corners of the grocery store's citrus display in the early part of the year. Costco and Trader Joe's are reliable retail sources, as well. Make and freeze lemon curd (page 67) for cheerful lemon meringue tartlettes at the drop of a hat.

Fresh apricots delivered from Frog Hollow Farm (froghollow.com) are indulgent, yes, but so delicious. Frog Hollow grows beautiful peaches, plums, and Meyer lemons, too.

ACKNOWLEDGMENTS

The idea for this book of flying pies was sparked in a telephone conversation with Lori Galvin, my superstar agent and the instigation behind most of my better ideas. At Grand Central, Karen Murgolo, editor extraordinaire, was enthusiastic from the start, particularly about the strudel, patient with my continual TOC shuffle, and unfailingly supportive and enthusiastic about these pie and pie-adjacent recipes. Morgan Hedden carried the torch forward, always happy to talk pie, tweak design elements, and kept the team focused on take-off. Again, I am grateful for the production precision of Tareth Mitch, copyedits from Deri Reed, and the design magic of Shubhani Sarkar.

I'm filled with gratitude when I see the photography, art direction, and food styling of Christopher Hirsheimer and Melissa Hamilton of Canal House. Working with them has been the best education and the most influential (and delicious) time. I rely on recipe tester Christine Rudalevige who baked pie after pie until the recipes worked every darn time; Mary Reilly, who watched over my recipe precision and conversions and regularly pulled me back from the edge; and Lauren Frager who taught me how to craft a better message.

I am grateful that Molly Pisula, my able kitchen assistant, found her way to my kitchen. Over several months, we had long, flour-filled days when making pies and empanadas, knishes and kolache. There were lovely lunches on the terrace, dogs that barked a lot, and dozens and dozens of blocks of dough made. I'm sorry about the 14 times you had to make fried pies, Molly, but the final recipe was worth it.

Thanks go to Alexandra Mudry Till who joined me in the kitchen to teach me how to strudel. Even in retirement, Gail Dosik provided the Phone-a-Pastry-Chef service she's made available for every book I've written. And Alex Levin taught me to salt the egg wash and right then changed my baking life forever.

Recipe development means making a recipe over and over and for this book, often that meant dozens of pies covering every surface of my condo by the end of a day. Molly took some home. I shared with the neighbors. I carried them to friends' homes. Finally, with 17 recipes left to test, it was time for a party—The Day of 400 Pies. Molly and I cooked for days and I opened my doors to friends who came to eat pie, who provided tasting notes, and offered up enthusiasm for all things pie. Adele and Kyle O'Dowd; Alejandra Owens; Aviva Goldfarb; Bonnie Benwick; Laura Kadetsky and Jonah and Abe Kaplan; Eris and John Norman; Jennifer Steinhauer and Jonathan Weisman; Anabeth Guthrie; Julia Devine; Julie Goos; Lisa Howard; Nancy Gale Dunn; Mara Bralove and Ari and Felix Fisher; Sonja Kubota Johannson; Chuck Pisula; Zach Levine and Jennifer Avellino; and Laura and Kevin Kumin. Buttery thanks to you all.

And for unflagging support, enthusiastic embrace of pie for dinner (again), and way too many last-minute grocery store runs, love and gratitude to my one true love, Dennis.

INDEX

ABOUT THE AUTHOR

CATHY BARROW is the IACP award winning author of *Mrs. Wheelbarrow's Practical Pantry: Recipes and Techniques for Year-Round Preserving* and *Pie Squared: Irresistibly Easy Sweet & Savory Slab Pies,* nominated for a James Beard Award, as well as a knitter, traveler, cook, teacher, and gardener. Published in the *New York Times,* the *Washington Post, Saveur, Serious Eats, Food52, The Local Palate, Garden & Gun, Southern Living,* NPR, and *National Geographic,* Cathy believes in the power of home cooking and the stories that connect us to food, culture, home, friends, and family.